THE
ISLE
OF MAN
TT COURSE

**the definitive guide to the world's
most demanding race circuit**

IAN LAWTON

TT Press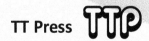

First published in 2022 by TT Press.

All enquiries to be directed to www.rspress.org.

A CIP catalogue record for this title is available from the British Library.

ISBN 978-0-9928163-9-1

Cover design by Ian Lawton.
Cover photograph of Ian Hutchinson at Conker Trees during the 2010 Superbike TT reproduced by kind permission of Dave Purves.
All other photographs © Ian Lawton unless otherwise stated.

DISCLAIMER The 'Rider's View' incorporated for each section of the course reflects the approach taken by highly experienced and talented racers. It *not* intended as a set of instructions to be followed by newcomers to the TT or MGP, who need to build considerable experience of the course before attempting to emulate faster competitors. Less still is it something for road riders to try to copy, even when traffic is one-way over the mountain during the TT. The author cannot be held responsible for anyone ignoring this disclaimer.

IAN LAWTON was first brought to the Isle of Man as a two-year-old, when he had the privilege to sit on the tank of Mike Hailwood's Norton in the winner's enclosure – his sister Pam and Mike were dating at the time.

His father Syd raced works Nortons, winning the Senior race at the 1953 NW200 with a new lap record before a bad accident at the Creg in practice for that year's TT ended his career. Turning to bike preparation, his Nortons and Enfields won the prestigious Thruxton 500-mile race for five years in a row from 1962 to 1966. But he's probably best remembered as the British importer of Italian Aermacchis from 1962. Apart from British championships, his bikes finished 2nd to Giacomo Agostini in the 1970 Junior, won several MGPs in the early 1970s, and took five consecutive Junior Classic MGP wins from 1987 to 1991.

Ian is enormously proud to have had Bob McIntyre as his godfather. He also raced his father's Aermacchis with no little success from the early 80s, including multiple Classic Race of the Year wins in the Lightweight, Junior and Senior classes, before moving on to modern Yamahas and then car racing in the Porsche Supercup. Meanwhile on the roads he had some good results at the Pre-TT Classic races on the Billown Circuit.

Born in 1959 and originally a qualified accountant, IT consultant and project manager, Ian has been writing books about ancient history and spiritual philosophy for over fifteen years. He now lives in the Isle of Man with his partner Mirka, where he builds classic café racers in his spare time. This is his first book about racing.

Some people maintain that modern MotoGP riders such as Valentino Rossi or Marc Marquez would blitz the TT course, and lap maybe 5 or even 10mph quicker than the current TT stars. I am not so sure.

From 1907 the earliest TTs were held on the shorter 'St John's Course', with the 'Mountain Course' not used until 1911. Much it was originally just cart tracks with multiple potholes and ruts, liberally strewn with stones, and with gates on the mountain that riders just had to hope had been opened before they arrived. It was only fully covered with tar by 1925, while the roads weren't closed for practice until 1928. Meanwhile, especially if dense fog was thrown into the mix, sheep and cows on the mountain were an additional hazard right up until 1934, when that entire stretch of road was fenced off.

Yet the first 60mph average lap speed was achieved by Jimmy Simpson in 1924 on still narrow and bumpy roads with poor surfaces, riding a machine with skinny frame and tyres and no suspension, against fierce rivals such as Howard Davies and Wal Handley. Incredibly he achieved the 70mph mark only two tears later, and 80mph in 1931, pushed now by riders of the calibre of Alec Bennett and Stanley Woods. With similar competition from Jimmy Guthrie and Harold Daniel, Freddie Frith then upped the record to over 90mph in 1937, before Daniel's 91mph set the following year stood for twelve years. Since then the road surface has been continuously improved and widened, and bumps and humps removed. Yet quite a few riders of modern 'classics', on far better machines, still fail to lap at this speed today – well over 80 years later!

Of course technical development, especially in terms of engines, tyres and suspension, is also a continuous process that eats away at lap times. This was especially true in a post-war period boasting star riders such as Bob Foster, Artie Bell, Bill Doran, Jack Brett, Johnny Lockett, Les Graham, Reg Armstrong, Bill Lomas, Ken Kavanagh and Ray Amm. Yet, although Geoff Duke came oh-so-close in 1955, it took nearly two decades for the inimitable Bob McIntyre to break the 100mph mark on his dustbin-faired Gilera in the 1957 Golden Jubilee Senior. All-time greats such as John Surtees, Jim Redman, Phil Read, Giacomo Agostini and Mike Hailwood then continued to raise speeds, with the latter setting a new record of nearly 109mph in the Diamond Jubilee Senior of 1967. But, while Mick Grant came close in 1975, it wasn't till the following year that John Williams finally achieved the first 110mph lap, aided by competition from the likes of Alex George, Tom Herron, Charlie and Peter Williams, Tony Rutter and Chas Mortimer.

After this the pace of record-breaking naturally slowed as speeds climbed, but stars such as Joey Dunlop, Graeme Crosby, Rob McElnea, Roger Marshall and Ron Haslam continued to push the envelope until, in 1989, Steve Hislop broke the 120mph barrier. He and riders of the calibre of Carl Fogarty, Phillip McCallen, Ian Lougher, Jim Moodie, David Jefferies and Adrian Archibald then continued to push speeds ever higher until finally, in 2007, John McGuinness achieved what had at one time seemed quite impossible – the first 130mph lap of the Mountain Course. Since then modern stars Steve Plater, Cameron Donald, Bruce Anstey, Michael Rutter, Ian Hutchinson, James Hiller, Guy Martin, Conor Cummins, Gary Johnson, Michael Dunlop, Dean Harrison and Peter Hickman have all played their part in raising the lap record above the 135mph mark. Is 140mph possible? History would suggest it probably is, at some point.

So, back to the MotoGP riders. It takes a very special kind of racer to even take on the challenge of the Mountain Course, let alone achieve greatness thereby. Just look at the stylised picture of Hutchinson accelerating through Conker Trees on the cover. His front wheel is a long way in the air with a significant degree of opposite lock to balance the bike as he powers through a kink in the road. Yes, short-circuit riders often get their bikes all 'crossed-up' and show almost unbelievable levels of skill and control. But not with solid brick walls, lampposts, trees and hedges on either side of a narrow, bumpy road where one split-second mistake may well spell disaster. I think that takes a very, very special kind of rider indeed. A hero in all senses of the word. Indeed, a true motorcycling god.

From a more personal perspective my father Syd gained just reward for his privateer efforts on the 'Continental Circus' with a first 'works' ride at the ripe old age of nearly forty, on a Moto Guzzi in the 1952 Lightweight. At 6'2" he was rather too tall for the bike, plus the ride was arranged at the last minute, but with little practice he took it to 3rd with the joint fastest lap. He was also first privateer home in the Junior on his 7R AJS. He then joined the works Norton team from mid 1952. After winning the Senior race at the 1953 NW200 and smashing the old lap record, he was at least in line for a podium in both the Junior and Senior TTs only a few weeks later. But the TT gods weren't smiling, and a bad accident at the Creg in practice ended his racing career.

Nevertheless, after a six-month stay in Nobles to recover from a massive twenty-seven fractures, he regrouped, set up a motorcycle dealership based in Southampton and, in the late 1950s, turned to bike preparation as an entrant-sponsor for a string of famous names. His Nortons and Enfields won the prestigious Thruxton 500-mile race for five years in a row from 1962 to 1966, but he's probably best remembered as the British importer of Italian Aermacchis, taking it on in 1962. Apart from British championships, on the Mountain Course his bikes finished 2nd to Giacomo Agostini in the 1970 Junior – with Alan Barnett missing the first ever magic 'ton' lap for a 350cc single by a mere whisker – and won several MGPs in the early 1970s before two-stroke dominance put an end to their competitiveness. But he then came back to take five consecutive Junior Classic MGPs from 1987 to 1991 with the late, great Richard Swallow in the saddle – and finally that magic 'ton' lap.

As if I wasn't lucky enough that the likes of Mike Hailwood and Phil Read were family friends, I'm incredibly proud that Bob McIntyre was my Godfather. He travelled all the way down from Scotland to be at my Christening in Southampton, and I used to race with a treasured silver spoon he gave me stuck down my right boot. An incredible competitor and even better person, he lost his life after an accident at Oulton Park in 1962. But what a legacy he left behind, especially at the TT, as we'll read in the forthcoming pages.

As for myself, I was mainly a British short-circuits racer, although I was lucky enough to have the chance to compete at several foreign GP tracks such as Assen and Monza too. My debut 'on the roads' came in the 1989 Pre-TT Classic on the Billown Circuit where, Aermacchi-mounted, I finished 2nd to Bill Swallow in the Junior race, coupled with a 4th on a Miles Trident in the Unlimited. The following year, in treacherous conditions and having beaten Bill at Monza the weekend before, I was too keen to repeat the feat. My bike gained the lead towards the end of the Junior race, but sadly I was no longer on it. That confirmed the view I'd always taken that I had neither the sense nor the ability to compete on the full Mountain Course, however much I respect those that do. But hopefully that doesn't preclude me from being able to write usefully and sensibly about it.

ACKNOWLEDGEMENTS My sincere thanks go to the experts whose on-board videos I have studied in compiling the 'Rider's View'; to my old friend and one-time rival Bill Swallow, for his valuable input on the lines to take on the more technical parts of the course; to my pal Mike Jones, the custodian of the McIntyre Collection, who reviewed the manuscript and suggested amendments based on his extensive knowledge of the TT; to Dave Purves and Gary Howlett for their permission to reproduce their photos of Ian Hutchinson and Bill Swallow respectively; and last, but by no means least, to my partner Mirka for her pictures of the experts, for correctly insisting that I should publish in colour not black and white, and for her unwavering love and support not just in this endeavour but in everything.

ADDITIONS AND CORRECTIONS In a book of this nature there will inevitably be some errors, omissions and changes over time. Please feel free to notify me of same via www.ianlawton.com, and if I agree they can then be incorporated into new editions. I am flexible on this because modern print-on-demand techniques don't require me to hold huge stocks that would then be made redundant.

Ian Lawton
April 2022

JIMMY SIMPSON 1931 80MPH

FREDDIE FRITH 1938 90MPH

BOB MCINTYRE 1957 100MPH
(© Mortons Archive)

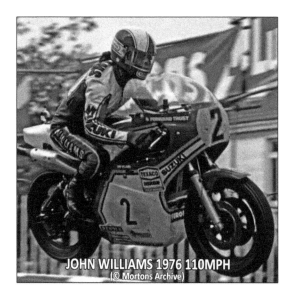

JOHN WILLIAMS 1976 110MPH
(© Mortons Archive)

STEVE HISLOP 1989 120MPH
(© motorcyclenews.com)

JOHN MCGUINNESS 2007 130MPH
(© Stephen Davison)

The author's father Syd crossing the line to win the 1953 NW200

The author's father Syd on the rostrum at the 1953 NW200, along with (L to R) Reg Armstrong, Bob McIntyre and Arthur Wheeler

The author's father Syd practising for the 1953 Senior TT on his works Norton

The author's father Syd with the winner's trophy at the 1962 Thruxton 500-mile race, flanked by riders Phil Read and Brian Setchell

The author with his godfather Bob McIntyre at his christening

The author's sister Pam with Mike Hailwood in the winner's enclosure at the 1961 TT

Alan Barnett in the winner's enclosure after finishing 2nd in the 1970 Junior on the Lawton Aermacchi, flanked by Giacomo Agostini (1st) and Paul Smart (3rd)

The author's father Syd with Richard Swallow, who took his Aermacchi to five consecutive wins in the Junior Classic MGP

The author winning the 1983 Senior Classic Race of the Year on father Syd's 422cc Aermacchi

The author finishing 2nd in the 1989 Pre-TT Classic at Billown on father Syd's 350cc Aermacchi

The author on the podium at Monza in 1990 with his great friend and rival Bill Swallow

The author on his FII Yamaha, tuned by Arnie Fletcher

My main sources for the 'Rider's View' of each section are primarily on-board videos on YouTube (for more details see 'Sources and Further Information' at the end). They show real race laps by some of the best-ever exponents of how to conquer the Mountain Course. Only one has any commentary so I've watched them ad infinitum, section by section, to dissect what the riders are doing at each point on the course in terms of speed, line and so on. They also cover a range of machines and years, although they're all 'modern'. In addition I have personally consulted a hugely experienced classic racer concerning the lines for some of the more technical sections of the course.

The experts are as follows, in no particular order (their photos are reproduced with the kind permission of Miroslawa Kurzydlowska, with the exception of the last, which is courtesy of Gary Howlett).

PLEASE NOTE THAT I HAVE NOT CONSULTED PETER, JOHN OR BRUCE PERSONALLY.

PETER HICKMAN is a professional motorcycle racer from Burton-upon-Trent. He is one of the few riders able to mix short circuits and the roads with great success, having competed in British Superbikes since 2006, with 6 wins, 21 podiums and a best of 4th in the championship in 2017. He made his TT debut in 2014 and set an outright lap record of 133.5mph in 2018. At the time of writing he has amassed 5 wins and 9 podiums. Born in 1987, he's still competing on the Island on modern machines.

My source is the on-board video of Peter during the final lap of the 2018 Senior, which he won on his 1000 BMW at an average of just under 133mph, and to which he subsequently added commentary.

JOHN MCGUINNESS is a professional motorcycle racer from Morecambe. Despite a fair degree of short circuit success as a 250cc British Champion who also competed in four Grand Prix in the late nineties, he's best known for his road racing exploits. At the TT he lies second on the all-time winners list, and was the first rider to break the 130mph barrier in 2007. He made his TT debut in 1996, achieved his first victory in 1999, and at the time of writing has amassed 23 wins and 47 podiums. Born in 1972, he's still competing on the Island on modern and classic machines.

My source is the on-board video of John during the first lap of the 2015 Senior, in which he finished 4th on his 1000 Honda at an average of just over 127mph. John has also provided various commentaries on how to approach the Mountain Course, both in videos and in written form – for example in 2007 in a book called 'TT 100', and again in an article for Motor Cycle News in 2014. I have incorporated elements of these where appropriate.

BRUCE ANSTEY is a professional motorcycle racer from New Zealand who specialises in road circuits, which is one of the reasons he now lives in Northern Ireland. A multiple TT winner who set an outright lap record in 2014, he made his TT debut in 1996, achieved his first victory in 2002, and at the time of writing has amassed 13 wins and 39 podiums. Born in 1969, and despite bouts of serious illness, he's still competing on the Island on classic machines.

My source is the on-board video of Bruce during the first lap of the 2011 Supersport Race 1, which he won on his 600 Honda at an average of just over 124mph.

 BILL SWALLOW is a retired teacher from Huddersfield. A classic racing demon on both road and short circuits, he first competed in the MGP in 1974 where, on his trusty Velocette, he ran up and along the top of the bank on the exit of Sarah's – a hard way to learn that it needs a late apex. He then went on to amass 9 wins in the Junior and Senior Classic between 1986 and 2003, coupled with a further 10 podiums. On modern machines, at the 1999 TT he finished 2nd in the Singles race on a Norton, and was similarly placed on the last lap of the Lightweight 400 when his Honda ran out of fuel at Governor's – he pushed in to finish 10th. He is still campaigning with a ridiculous turn of speed, in the Pre-TT Classic and elsewhere, at as age when most people have long since put their feet up.

I have discussed the more technical parts of the course with Bill, especially those corners with multiple apexes, or where unusual lines have to be taken to prepare for the next bend (his advice about the line at Handley's came from none other than the great John Surtees). Although he's mainly a classic racer, these lines apply equally well to modern machines.

how to use this guide

I have split the circuit into FIVE SECTORS of roughly equal length. Then for each SECTION within it I include the following:

THE COURSE The shape and speed of the section, the reason for its name and any former names, and any key landmarks. I use my own standardised terminology as follows:

- 'Left' or 'right' means a proper corner or bend.

- 'Kink' means the bike is laid in that direction only for a very short time.

- 'Sweep' means the bike is laid over for a lengthy period round one smooth curve.

- 'Multiple apex left/right' means two or more bends that can be taken as one without lifting the bike up. All apexes should be hit unless otherwise stated.

- 'Double left/right' means two bends in a row but the bike must be lifted in between.

- 'Crest' means a brow where at least the front end will come up, while a 'jump' means both wheels will be off the ground.

- 'Main' means the one of the bends for which the section is noted, which may in some cases be preceded or followed by one or more unnamed bends or kinks.

- 'Fast' typically means 5th or 6th gear, possibly flat out.

- 'Medium' typically means 3rd or 4th gear.

- 'Slow' typically means 1st or 2nd gear.

Note that the course uses normal roads under heavy everyday use, and is therefore notoriously bumpy, despite constant efforts to maintain or improve the surface. Consequently I only emphasise those sections that are especially bad.

THE RIDER'S VIEW How to ride that section, collated from videos of and commentary by the aforementioned experts. Again I use my own standardised terminology as follows:

- 'Ease' the throttle may involve a dab on the brakes as well, usually staying in the same gear but occasionally going down one.

- 'Reduce speed' means changing down one or more gears and almost certainly some braking as well.

- 'Hard' acceleration or braking is self explanatory. The former will typically mean the front coming up too, sometimes for a fair time.

Note also that:

- The consistent advice from all riders is to apex the corners on the Mountain Course late. Consequently I only tend to emphasise those that should be apexed especially late or, if part of a sequence, not at all.

- In most places I've tried to distinguish between e.g. easing the throttle on a superbike compared to being flat out on a less powerful bike. Of course in some places instructions to ease or reduce speed will be redundant on a slower, e.g. classic, bike.

- When the front rises over any of the more severe crests it may be necessary to ease, or at least use the rear brake to control the lift.

- I have deliberately made no mention of braking or peel-off points. This is because a) they will vary depending on the speed of the bike and rider, and b) landmarks change over time, so providing details can be misleading at best and downright dangerous at worst. Riders will have their own ways of determining these things.

NOTABLE EVENTS These typically include retirements or accidents involving better-known riders who were in contention for a TT win or podium (I haven't included the MGP due to prioritisation and space constraints). In the case of accidents they often recovered or weren't too badly hurt. However, given the challenging nature of the course, it's only right that we also pay our respects to some of those who have sadly lost their lives on various parts of the circuit over the years.

CHANGES Information on road widening, hump removal and other improvements over the years. Resurfacing is not mentioned unless recent. The changes are typically made over the winter of the year quoted and into the spring of the following year.

SPECTATING Outlines of where to watch the action. Note the following:

- The majority of viewing areas have limited capacity so, especially during TT race week, early arrival is essential.

- Viewing areas cannot be accessed when the roads are closed, unless otherwise stated.

- 'B' roads tend to be narrow, single track and can become clogged. Also parking can be a problem in many of the areas mentioned, so it's best to ask for advice beforehand. It goes without saying that a bike takes up less space than a car.

- There will be charges in a number of the places mentioned, while remoter areas have no facilities.

- In some areas with trackside fields and banks, asking permission from the landowner is recommended. Again, if in doubt, ask for advice.

- The 'Access Road', which provides a route to the inside of some southerly parts of the course when roads are closed, runs underneath the bridge at Braddan.

More details are provided on several websites mentioned under 'Sources and Further Information' at the end – although note that, sadly but for safety and insurance reasons, more restrictions are being put in place ever year.

PHOTOS At the end of each sector I include photos of the key parts of each section. They are taken from the racing line looking in the direction of the course. The numbering merely reflects the order of the photos for that section.

why this guide is needed

One of the reasons I decided to prepare this book is that every TT course guide I've ever consulted, whether in map or book form, always seemed to have different names for some corners, or to leave some out, leading me to ask: is there a definitive view of the course? I am not sure there ever has been, or even can be, but my main objective is to try to get as close as possible to it.

That having been said, what have been the most comprehensive guides up until now?

SILJA'S TT COURSE KNOWLEDGE

This online guide prepared by Swedish enthusiast Jan-Ake Siljestrom (see 'Sources and Further Information') is far more detailed than anything else I've encountered, especially in incorporating former and alternative names for each section, on which I have at times drawn. What is more we both attempt to produce a more comprehensive guide than our predecessors in terms of clarifying additional unnamed bends or kinks that precede or follow the named sections, although not in exactly the same way.

But Silja's approach also differs significantly from mine, not least in as much as, although he refers to several videos, he has no pictures – whereas I decided early on to photograph pretty much every twist and turn to match the detail of the commentary. I also go into more detail on the 'Rider's View' of each section, using a broader range of expert input and adopting standard terminology for road shapes, speeds and so on, as described under 'How to Use This Guide'. Finally by including the 'Notable Events' that have occurred in each section, I hope to bring the guide to life and make for more interesting reading.

By contrast Silja provides extensive information on name derivations, on distances, mileages and course markers, and on memorials, none of which I include. He also has far more detail on spectator access and facilities than I do.

It is a case of 'horses for courses', but I can thoroughly recommend his site.

RAY KNIGHT'S BOOKS

This highly experienced and respected former TT racer produced two course guides in book form, one in 1974 and an updated version in 1991 (again see 'Sources and Further Information'). Ray did concentrate on the rider's perspective, and included a great many pictures – although in black-and-white rather than colour – so in some respects at least I am attempting to emulate him. However both of these books been out of print for some time, while even the most recent was produced more than thirty years ago, when bikes, lap times and the course itself were quite different in many respects. So it's no criticism of Ray's fine work to suggest an update might be required.

One of the problems I've faced, and undoubtedly Ray or his publishers would have too, is how to incorporate all the pictures one wants for completeness, while keeping them in sync with the relevant text, yet still avoiding large blank areas all over the place. There are some fairly glaring omissions in Ray's otherwise excellent photos, and I suspect this may be the reason. I have wrestled with this problem and, because for me completeness is everything, I've chosen the solution of, for each sector of the course, laying out all the text and then the photos on the following pages. I felt this would be better than placing all the photos at the back, but it still largely resolves the problem of too many blank spaces.

I have tried to the best of my ability, then, to create perhaps the most comprehensive, up-to-date, illustrated guide to the TT Mountain Course, using the most standardised naming and terminology, ever produced. But whether I've succeeded or not... well, that's for you to judge.

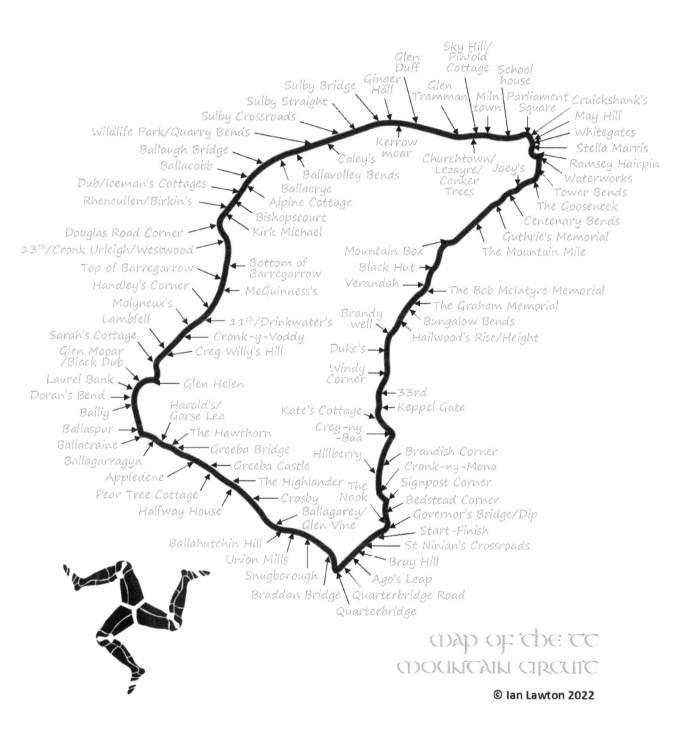

Sky Hill/
Pinfold
Cottage

Glen
Duff

School
house

Ginger
Hall

Glen
Tramman

Miln
town

Parliament
Square

Cruickshank's

Sulby Bridge

May Hill

Sulby Straight

Whitegates

Sulby Crossroads

Stella Marris

Wildlife Park/Quarry Bends

Kerrow
moar

Ramsey Hairpin

Ballaugh Bridge

Caley's

Churchtown/
Lezayre/
Conker
Trees

Joey's

Waterworks

Ballacobb

Ballavolley Bends

Tower Bends

Dub/Iceman's Cottages

Ballacrye

The Gooseneck

Rhencullen/Birkin's

Alpine Cottage

Centenary Bends

Bishopscourt

Guthrie's Memorial

Douglas Road Corner

Kirk Michael

Mountain Box

The Mountain Mile

13th/Cronk Urleigh/Westwood

Black Hut

Top of Barregarrow

Bottom of
Barregarrow

Verandah

The Bob McIntyre Memorial

Handley's Corner

McGuinness's

The Graham Memorial

Molyneux's

Brandy
well

Bungalow Bends

Lambfell

11th/Drinkwater's

Hailwood's Rise/Height

Sarah's Cottage

Cronk-y-Voddy

Glen Mooar
/Black Dub

Creg Willy's Hill

Duke's

Laurel Bank

Glen Helen

Windy
Corner

Doran's Bend

33rd

Ballig

Harold's/
Gorse Lea

Kate's Cottage

Keppel Gate

Ballaspur

The Hawthorn

Creg-ny
-Baa

Brandish Corner

Ballacraine

Greeba Bridge

Hillberry

Cronk-ny-Mona

Ballagarragyn

Greeba Castle

Signpost Corner

Appledene

The Highlander

The
Nook

Bedstead Corner

Pear Tree Cottage

Crosby

Governor's Bridge/Dip

Halfway House

Ballagarey/
Glen Vine

Start-Finish

Ballahutchin Hill

St Ninian's Crossroads

Union Mills

Bray Hill

Snugborough

Ago's Leap

Braddan Bridge

Quarterbridge Road

Quarterbridge

map of the tt
mountain circuit

© Ian Lawton 2022

5 BRANDYWELL TO FINISH

The Start-Finish

Situated on Glencrutchery Road in Douglas, the road curves very gently left with the pit lane and main grandstands on the left. In the vicinity are the race offices, scrutineering bays, holding area, winner's enclosure and paddock. This is now the sole commentary point.

THE RIDER'S VIEW

Hard on through here, although coming into the pits requires hard braking into the stop line that limits speed.

NOTABLE EVENTS

1952 Having won the Senior for the last two years, Geoff Duke retires his Norton from the lead on lap four. But his team mate Reg Armstrong has more luck when his chain breaks just as he crosses the line to win.

1955 On the third lap of the Senior a now Gilera-mounted Geoff Duke is credited with the first 100mph lap, only for it to be downgraded to 99.97 shortly after.

1967 Mike Hailwood screams through in the lead of the Junior. On his 297cc Honda 6 he has set a new *outright* lap record of nearly 108mph from a standing start, before winning comfortably from Giacomo Agostini's MV. He goes on to raise it to nearly 109mph in the Senior, although in a much tighter duel with his rival.

1977 The new Formula One race is introduced to compensate for the loss of world championship status in the other races. At the end of the third lap Ducati-mounted leader Roger Nicholls pits for fuel while returnee Phil Read goes straight through on his Honda, taking the win when the race is stopped at the end of the next lap due to worsening weather.

1978 After he crosses the line in the Formula One for the most popular win in TT history, returnee Mike Hailwood's Ducati is found to have suffered a bevel gear failure that moments later would have forced his retirement.

1979 In an unforgettable Classic Mike Hailwood, this time Suzuki-mounted, leads by 0.8s going into the final lap having clawed back Honda-mounted Alex George's advantage. However Alex breaks everyone's heart with a brilliant final lap to deny Mike in his final TT, albeit he had earlier won the Senior.

1981 Graeme Crosby's Suzuki is forced to start at the back of the field after chain problems yet, with no time allowance, he still manages a brilliant 3rd behind the Hondas of Ron Haslam and Joey Dunlop. After Haslam has received the winner's garland Suzuki protest, the time allowance is approved and Crosby declared the winner. Honda then make their own protest for the Classic, with their bikes and riders all in black.

1990 In the Junior Steve Hislop loses time in the pits when his Honda's fuel cap is dropped into the fairing during a terrific dice with Ian Lougher's Yamaha. Perhaps unexpectedly the latter takes his first TT win by just 1.8s with an astounding last lap at nearly 118mph, a 250cc record that will last for many years. Hislop will later describe that last lap as the hardest he ever rode around the Mountain Course.

2002 Despite a 5s penalty for overshooting the stop box, Suzuki-mounted Ian Lougher finishes only 22s adrift of similarly mounted David Jefferies in the fastest-ever Senior. With the 2001 meeting having been cancelled due to 'foot and mouth' disease, this gives Jefferies a unique three-years-in-a-row treble, this time also winning the Formula One and Production 1000.

2007 Appropriately in Centenary year, Honda-mounted John McGuinness becomes the first man to break the 130mph barrier as he completes the second lap of the Senior. He goes on to win comfortably from similarly-mounted Guy Martin and Ian Hutchinson.

2019 In the Senior BMW-mounted Peter Hickman has a healthy lead over Kawasaki rival Dean Harrison as he comes in for his second pit stop. However overheating problems slow him and Harrison goes on to take the win. Hickman just hangs on to 2nd but his consolation is a Superbike-Superstock-Supersport 2 treble.

CHANGES

1926 The road is widened and a wooden grandstand complex constructed.

1986 A new brick double-grandstand and race control tower are erected, and the pit lane widened.

2021 The famous manual scoreboards on the right of the course, operated by Boy Scouts, are taken down.

2022 The pit lane is lengthened with the addition of extra refuelling cubicles.

SPECTATING

Tickets are required for the 1000-seater grandstands but they provide all the close-up action from pit stops, close finishes and garlanding ceremonies.

ST NINIAN'S CROSSROADS

A fast left kink with the church on the left, at the start of a steep descent.

THE RIDER'S VIEW

Flat through here, hugging the right past the start-finish and through a slight right kink to line the left kink up, after which the bike becomes airborne as the road drops away.

NOTABLE EVENTS

1978 Mac Hobson and Kenny Birch sadly lose their lives after an accident in Sidecar A.

CHANGES

1920 The startline is relocated here from the top of Bray Hill.

High-speed viewing from either side, with a footbridge linking the two.

BRAY hill

A fast, steep descent with slight right-left kinks on the way down and a fuller right kink at the bottom.

THE RIDER'S VIEW

Watch out for the crest after the first right kink, then stay to the left before diving late into the dip to minimise the bumps, staying a little out from the kerb as the suspension bottoms out. Flat all the way through, maybe even on a superbike. This section needs full commitment to avoid losing time, even on the first lap right after the start or after a pit stop, both with a full fuel tank and fresh tyres.

CHANGES

1914 The startline is moved from Quarterbridge Road to the top of Bray.

SPECTATING

The wide junction with Stoney Road on the left of the dip provides spectacular action, with views both back up the hill to the right and on up the hill to the left, where other narrower junctions abound.

AGO's leap

A straight, steep rise from the bottom of Bray incorporating two crests. The first is named after a famous photo of MV-mounted Giacomo Agostini was taken here in the 1970 Senior.

THE RIDER'S VIEW

Flat through here despite the crests.

quarterbridge road

The road drops now through a fast left kink at the junction with Alexander Drive on the left sometimes referred to as Eyreton Corner, followed by another crest. The distinctive, post-modern Nook Café, built in the 1930s but sadly now closed for many years, is located on the left at the bottom.

THE RIDER'S VIEW

Reduce speed before the kink and again before the crest, then hard downhill braking.

NOTABLE EVENTS

1953 Having already won the Ultra Lightweight, Les Graham sadly loses his life after an accident in the Senior on his MV. He was leading the 1949 Senior when his works AJS expired, although he went on to become the inaugural 500cc world champion that year, before switching to MV in 1951 and taking the runner-up spot in the Senior.

CHANGES

1911-13 The startline is initially here on the flat section, with Selborne Drive on the left used as an assembly area.

1954 The steep descent at the bottom is widened.

1979 Much of the road is reprofiled.

QUARTERBRIDGE

A wide, slow right at a major road junction. The pub of the same name that sits on the far side sadly remained closed after the Covid lockdown of 2020-21.

THE RIDER'S VIEW

Take special care on entry and exit with a full tank of fuel and cold tyres, and the possibility of diesel spills on the road too. Accelerate hard only after the apex as the road tightens a little on the exit, and then on along the following straight, which includes a crest.

NOTABLE EVENTS

1953 Gilera-mounted Geoff Duke slides out of the lead of the Senior on lap four.

1971 In heavy rain Barry Sheene slips off his Suzuki and out of 2nd on the second lap of the Ultra Lightweight, in his only appearance at the TT. Chas Mortimer's Yamaha takes the win.

1973 Jack Findlay retires his Suzuki from 2nd in the Formula 750, handing an easy win to Peter Williams' monocoque-framed Norton.

CHANGES

1912 The road is widened considerably.

SPECTATING

Plenty of room to watch from the left of the bend.

BRADDAN BRIDGE

The Joey Dunlop Foundation building lies ahead on the entry to a slow, wide, left-right S-bend, with the bridge over the river Dhoo in the middle and two churches on the left on the exit.

THE RIDER'S VIEW

Reduce speed including through a left kink on the entry, and again be careful through the main left on cold tyres, apexing it late so as to be able to accelerate hard through the right. Also beware the jutting curb of a left kink on the exit.

NOTABLE EVENTS

1981 Chris Guy crashes his private Suzuki in the restarted Senior. The previous day he 'won' the two-lap original that was stopped due to appalling weather and declared void –

possibly after pressure from embarrassed works teams.

2018 On the first lap of the Superstock BMW-mounted Peter Hickman outbrakes himself on the entry and runs on, leaving him 8th at Glen Helen. He then storms through the field to take the lead on lap three from similarly mounted Michael Dunlop and the Kawasaki of Dean Harrison. Dunlop responds, but with a superb last lap Hickman goes on to take a hard-fought first win. He goes on to do the same in the Senior after Harrison had led throughout, snatching his second win with an epic first 135mph lap on the final circuit.

CHANGES

1922 The approach road is widened.

1926 The bends are substantially widened.

2007 Further widening is undertaken.

SPECTATING

On the left on the exit a 400-seater grandstand lies in front of the first church, with a spectator area in front of the second, both with views through the entire section and accessible from Saddle Road.

SNUGBOROUGH

A fast left kink near the entrance to the trading estate of the same name on the right.

THE RIDER'S VIEW

Flat through a previous left kink and on through the main one, but possibly ease slightly for the crest after it.

NOTABLE EVENTS

2019 Daley Mathison sadly loses his life after an accident in the Superbike. He achieved podiums in the TT Zero in 2016, 2017 and 2018.

CHANGES

1976 The road is widened.

UNION MILLS

A downhill approach into a medium right and double-apex left, with the Railway pub on the left on the entry. On the right on the exit a convenience store was once the home of the young Bee Gees.

THE RIDER'S VIEW

Flat through a right kink on the approach, then reduce speed for a left kink and into the main right, pulling the bike over to change direction for the long left and accelerating from about halfway round this. Potentially sacrifice speed through the first part to get good drive out of the second and on up the following climb, which is one of the most important elements of a fast lap.

NOTABLE EVENTS

1948 While leading the Senior on the fifth lap, Omobono Tenni stops to make adjustments to his Moto Guzzi. He eventually finishes 9th.

1983 On the fourth lap of the Junior 350 Con Law retires his Yamaha after a close scrap with similarly mounted Phil Mellor, who goes on to win. Law however has the consolation of a comfortable win in the Junior 250 on his EMC.

1991 Pre-race favourites Steve Hislop and Ian Lougher are forced to retire their Honda and Yamaha machines within 100 yards of each other on lap two of the Junior. This leaves Robert Dunlop, Phillip McCallen and Brian Reid to contest the win, the former prevailing.

SPECTATING

The Railway Inn is accessible via Cronk Road and has a raised beer garden. On the exit there are spectator areas in front of both the Church and Memorial Halls, reachable via Strang Road and the Access Road.

Ballahutchin Hill

A long, straight climb out of Union Mills, with a crest then a fast right kink after which the road descends briefly then climbs again at the top.

THE RIDER'S VIEW

Flat all the way, tucking in as much as possible.

NOTABLE EVENTS

2007 Having set a new lap record from a standing start, leader Nick Crowe's outfit expires on the second lap of Sidecar B, handing victory to Dave Molyneux.

SPECTATING

Fields and hedges line the course, especially on the left.

Ballagarey – Glen Vine

A fast right kink on the entry to Glen Vine village, formerly known as Elm Bank.

THE RIDER'S VIEW

Nicknamed Ballascary, this is one of the most serious challenges on the course because again good exit speed is essential for the fast section that follows, but ease on the way in just as the road starts to ascend again at the top of the previous straight, possibly dropping down a gear on a superbike. After a right kink the following straight includes several crests.

NOTABLE EVENTS

1989 Phil Hogg sadly loses his life after an accident practising for the Lightweight. In 1987 he finished 2nd in the Senior Newcomers MGP. The following year he won the open race at the Southern 100, and set the first sub-20 minute lap while leading the Senior MGP before coming off at Cronk-ny-Mona on the second lap.

1997 Colin Gable sadly loses his life after an accident practising for the Senior. He won the Senior Newcomers MGP in 1987 before finishing 5th in the 1989 Production 1300, 3rd in the Junior in 1995 and 4th in each of the Production and Junior in 1996.

2010 Paul Dobbs sadly loses his life after an accident in Supersport 2, having first competed at the TT in 1999 and finished 6th in the Lightweight 400 the following year. Meanwhile Guy Martin has an infamous crash while challenging for the lead of the Senior when his Honda becomes a fireball and an internet video sensation.

CHANGES

1955 The bend is eased.

CROSBY

A fast left kink in the village, sometimes referred to as Church Hall Corner, is followed by a crossroads, then the road ascends gently on the exit as it passes the Crosby pub on the right and on up the straight that follows.

THE RIDER'S VIEW

Line up carefully for the left kink, which is flat maybe even on a superbike, and watch out for the jutting curb on the subsequent slight right kink. Another left kink precedes the pub.

NOTABLE EVENTS

1972 Chris Vincent retires his Munch-URS from 2nd on the second lap of the 500 Sidecar and, after leader Klaus Enders' BMW expires a lap later at Ramsey, Siggi Shauzu takes his seventh win and the first ever 500-750 double.

2003 David Jefferies sadly loses his life after an accident practising for the Senior. His numerous achievements as a nine-time TT winner are mentioned throughout this book.

CHANGES

1922 The road through the village is widened.

SPECTATING

The large garden of the pub provides high-speed action.

the halfway house

Still fast and straight, the spectacular Crosby Jump is at the top of the hill. After this on the left lies the former pub after which this section is named, also briefly called The Wagon and Horses, which is now a private house. The road descends gently from this point.

THE RIDER'S VIEW

Nearing the top of the hill keep to the right where the crest is less severe, possibly easing on a superbike, then hard on through slight right-left kinks. Also beware cross-winds.

1962 Two banks are removed to straighten the road.

Fields and hedges line the course near the jump, especially on the left.

The highlander

Still fast and straight, named after the former pub on the right, which then became a restaurant and is now a private house. At one time this was the site of the official speed trap.

THE RIDER'S VIEW

Still hard on, straightening out some slight kinks.

CHANGES
1935 The road is widened.
1954 The jump is flattened out.

Pear Tree Cottage

A fast, downhill, triple-apex left named after the house on the right.

THE RIDER'S VIEW

Reduce speed on entry, taking care because the brakes haven't been used for some time, then accelerate briefly.

Greeba Castle

A medium left-right S-bend. On the right lies the Gothic-style castle built in the Victorian era from which it derives its name. It was once occupied by the famous novelist Hall Caine, after whom this section was also once known.

THE RIDER'S VIEW

Reduce speed again for the left, hugging the right curb before peeling in, then accelerate hard only after the apex of the right because it's adverse camber and the exit tightens.

NOTABLE EVENTS

1997 Danny Shimmin sadly loses his life after an accident practising for the Junior Classic, riding the ex-Richard Swallow Lawton Aermacchi. In the MGP he finished 3rd in the Lightweight in 1971 and 1972 before winning it in 1976, coupled with runner-up spot in the Senior. Moving up to the TT he finished 6th in the Formula One in 1982, while from 1987 he took numerous top-six finishes in both the Junior and Senior Classics.

CHANGES
1912 The road is widened considerably.
1935 The bends are eased.

Appledene

A medium-fast left and double-apex right. The cottage from which it derives its name used to lie on the left but was demolished in 1953. The second right is also named after Cronk Dhoo Farm on the right.

THE RIDER'S VIEW

A slight left kink and a crest on the entry can be taken flat, then ease for the main left and into the first right, before driving hard through it and on through the second right.

CHANGES

1954 The road is widened.

GREEBA BRIDGE

A medium left through a bridge over the river of the same name.

THE RIDER'S VIEW

Straighten the kinks on the preceding straight, then reduce speed on the entry before hard on again.

NOTABLE EVENTS

2009 In Sidecar 1 Nick Crowe retires from the lead on lap two, leaving Dave Molyneux to take a comfortable fourteenth win.

CHANGES

1938 The road is widened.
1960s Further widening is undertaken.

The hawthorn

A fast straight named after the former pub on the left, which is now a restaurant.

THE RIDER'S VIEW

Flat through here.

NOTABLE EVENTS

1995 Having triumphed in the Ultra Lightweight for the last three years, Honda-mounted Joey Dunlop retires on the opening lap with a 'cold seizure' – caused by too much duct tape on his radiator.

Viewing is possible from the restaurant car park.

harold's – gorse Lea

A right kink followed by a fast right. The former was renamed in 2019 after the owner of Knock Breck Farm on the left, Harold Leece, who for many years provided hospitality for spectators in his garden.

THE RIDER'S VIEW
Flat through a preceding left kink and the first right, and through the second except perhaps just feather on a superbike, leaving its apex very late so as not to run out of road on the exit.

CHANGES
1953 The road is widened.

SPECTATING
The hedges between the two rights provide one of the most stunning viewing spots, with access via Kennaa Road (B) and a field for a car park.

Ballagarraghyn

A fast straight but with a slight left kink, named after the adjacent farm.

THE RIDER'S VIEW
Flat through here, including over a crest before the kink.

CHANGES
1954 The original jump is flattened out.

SPECTATING
Fields and hedges line the course on the left.

THE START-FINISH

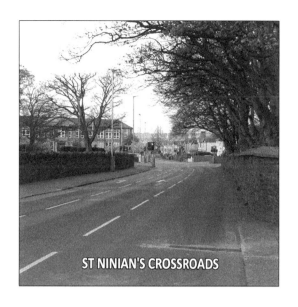

ST NINIAN'S CROSSROADS

BRAY HILL 1

BRAY HILL 2

BRAY HILL 3

AGO'S LEAP 1

AGO'S LEAP 2

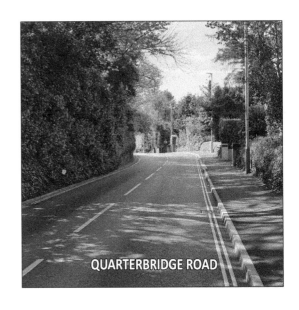

QUARTERBRIDGE ROAD

QUARTERBRIDGE 1

QUARTERBRIDGE 2

BRADDAN BRIDGE 1

BRADDAN BRIDGE 2

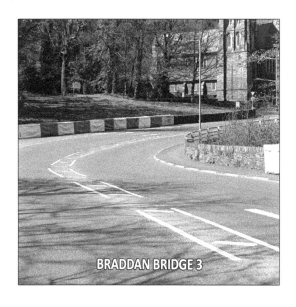

BRADDAN BRIDGE 3

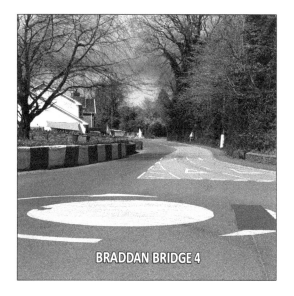

BRADDAN BRIDGE 4

SNUGBOROUGH

UNION MILLS 1

UNION MILLS 2

UNION MILLS 3

UNION MILLS 4

UNION MILLS 5

BALLAHUTCHIN HILL

BALLAGAREY

CROSBY 1

CROSBY 2

THE HALFWAY HOUSE

THE HIGHLANDER

PEAR TREE COTTAGE

GREEBA CASTLE 1

GREEBA CASTLE 2

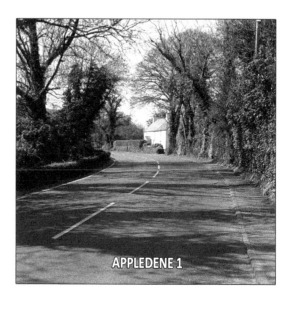

APPLEDENE 1

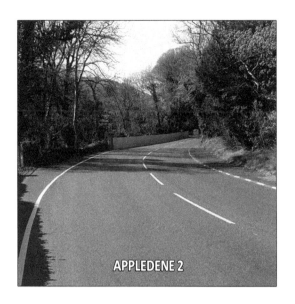

APPLEDENE 2

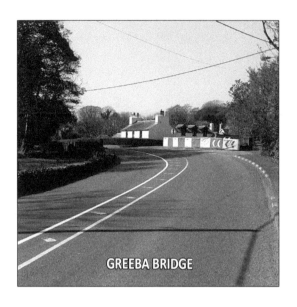

GREEBA BRIDGE

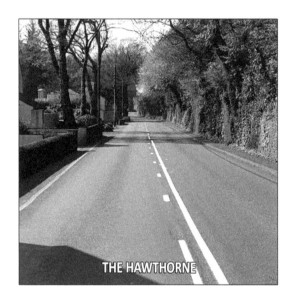

THE HAWTHORNE

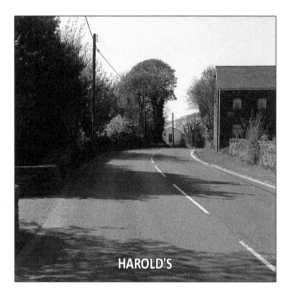

HAROLD'S

GORSE LEA

BALLAGARRAGHYN

Ballacraine

A slow right where the road carries straight on to Peel or left to Foxdale. Named after the former pub on the outside of the corner, now a private house.

THE RIDER'S VIEW

Hard braking on the entry, then hard on up the gentle climb on the exit.

NOTABLE EVENTS

1935 George Formby crashes through the pub doorway in the film 'No Limit'.

1947 Freddie Frith crashes his Moto Guzzi practising for the Senior and is unable to race.

1968 Georg Auerbacher retires from the lead of the Sidecar on the last lap, letting in relative newcomer Siggi Shauzu for the win, both BMW mounted.

2008 John Goodall sadly loses his life after an accident in the Junior Classic. In the MGP he finished 3rd in both the 1973 Senior and the Junior of the following year, before winning the inaugural Senior Classic in 1983, followed by no less than twelve podium finishes in this and the Junior Classic.

1980 Ian Richards retires his Yamaha on the final lap of the Senior after an epic race-long duel with Graeme Crosby, who goes on to win on his Suzuki.

SPECTATING

Seating is available on the left of the entry, accessible from the A3 Curragh Road from Foxdale or from the A1 from Peel.

Ballaspur

A medium, uphill left followed by a right kink and two medium rights.

THE RIDER'S VIEW

Ease before the left, then drive hard through the kink and the two rights, although not using all of the road on the exit of the first.

NOTABLE EVENTS

2003 Richard 'Milky' Quayle has a well-publicised accident captured by both spectator and on-board footage. Two years earlier, with victory in the Lightweight 400, he became the first Manxman to win a solo TT for over thirty years.

Ballig

A straight with slight kinks that at one time contained a hump-backed bridge, now much reduced.

Straighten the preceding kinks then start reducing speed just before the bridge.

NOTABLE EVENTS

1948 Les Graham's AJS expires while leading the Senior on the fourth lap.

1951 On the third lap of the Lightweight Fergus Anderson retires his Moto Guzzi while leading, having set a new lap record.

1982 Mick Grant crashes his Suzuki while leading the Senior. Similarly mounted newcomer Norman Brown goes on to take the win.

1999 Having broken the seven-year-old absolute lap record from a standing start, at just under 125mph, Jim Moodie is forced to retire his Honda on the second lap of the Senior with a shredded rear tyre. Yamaha-mounted David Jefferies goes on to complete a Senior-Formula One-Production treble.

2000 In a close Formula One battle with Joey Dunlop's Honda, David Jefferies is forced to retire his Yamaha on lap five. His consolation is a treble to follow up the same feat in the previous year, this time winning the Senior, Production and Junior 600. Dunlop also goes on to achieve a treble, winning the Formula One, Lightweight 250 and Ultra Lightweight to take his tally to 26 wins; but he will never return to his beloved Mountain Course, tragically losing his life at an obscure meeting in Estonia only a few weeks later.

2012 Michael Dunlop retires his Yamaha from a comfortable lead on the third lap of Supersport 1, leaving an epic scrap to be fought out between the Hondas of Bruce Anstey, Cameron Donald and Gary Johnson, the former coming out on top by just 0.77s.

CHANGES

1935 The original bridge is removed and the road widened, reducing lap times by between 3s and 5s.

1960s Further widening is undertaken.

SPECTATING

From the junction with the A20 Poortown Road from Peel, with parking at nearby Tynwald Mills.

DORAN'S BEND

A medium-fast triple-apex left named after Bill Doran, who had an accident here practising for the 1950 Junior. Glen Helen House is set back on the right on the exit.

THE RIDER'S VIEW

Make the first apex then drive hard through the remainder, making sure you can cut back to the left of the road towards the end to get ready for the next right.

NOTABLE EVENTS

1989 Phil Mellor sadly loses his life after an accident in the Production 1300. A multiple British champion in various production classes, he followed victory in the 1978

Newcomer's Lightweight MGP with TT wins in the 1983 Junior, 1984 Production 250 and 1986 Production B, as well as four other podiums.

Laurel Bank

A medium-slow right-right-left-right combination.

THE RIDER'S VIEW

Reduce speed for the first right but stay out from the apex, then on the power again briefly and apex the second before easing for the left, on the power again briefly through a slight left kink then reduce speed again for the final right. Do not put the power on too early because it tightens on the exit.

NOTABLE EVENTS

1951 Norton-mounted Harry Hinton crashes out of 2nd on the third lap of the Junior.

1962 Having already taken 3rd in the Ultra Lightweight and Lightweight, Tom Phillis sadly loses his life after an accident on the second lap of the Junior while lying 3rd on his Honda; in the meantime his great friend, MV-mounted Gary Hocking, continues oblivious in an epic duel with team mate Mike Hailwood, the latter prevailing by just 5s. As for Phillis, after a 4th in the 1960 Senior, the following year he finished 2nd in the Lightweight and 3rd in the Ultra Lightweight and Senior, before going on to become the 125cc world champion.

2010 Conor Cummins is forced to retire his Kawasaki on the fifth lap of the Superbike, having come close to a new outright lap record from a standing start and with a commanding lead until a slow second pit stop.

CHANGES

1931 The road is widened.

1935 Further widening takes place.

1973 The road is smoothed out by eliminating humps and bumps.

SPECTATING

A grass bank lines the course on the left of the exit, accessible via the back roads off the A20 Poortown Road from Peel.

Black Dub – Glen Mooar

A medium double-apex left followed by a longer double-apex right. The Black Dub lodge is on the right on entry.

THE RIDER'S VIEW

Straighten the preceding series of right-left-right kinks while hard on, then reduce speed into the main left before accelerating hard from between the two rights and through a left kink that follows.

NOTABLE EVENTS

1985 Rob Vine sadly loses his life after an accident in the Senior, having taken seven top-ten finishes, with a best of 6th in the 1983 Junior.

1994 Mark Farmer sadly loses his life after an accident practising for the Senior, having secured six top-six finishes, with a best of 4th in the 1990 Supersport 600. Back to 1994 and in the latter event Yamaha-mounted Jim Moodie crashes out of the lead on lap three, handing the win to similarly mounted Iain Duffus.

CHANGES

1935 The road is widened.

1973 The road is smoothed out by eliminating humps and bumps.

Glen helen

A fast left followed by a medium left-right and finally a medium-slow double-apex left, one of the former commentary points. On the right on the exit is the former hotel and pub of the same name, which is now the Swiss Chalet restaurant.

THE RIDER'S VIEW

Ease slightly for the first left then reduce speed for the second, power on briefly through the right then reduce speed again for the final left. Apex the second left late so as to come out not too far to the right of the road on the exit because of the adverse camber.

NOTABLE EVENTS

1929 Henry Tyrell-Smith crashes his Rudge while leading on the third lap of the Senior, but remounts to finish 3rd with three cracked ribs.

1962 Mike Hailwood retires his private EMC from 2nd on the final lap of the Ultra Lightweight, allowing the all-conquering Hondas a clean sweep.

1987 Steve Hislop has a comfortable lead on the fifth lap of the Junior when his Yamaha expires, leaving EMC-mounted Brian Reid and Eddie Laycock to fight it out for the win, the latter prevailing. Hislop will however win his first TT, the Formula Two, later in the week.

1996 Rob Holden sadly loses his life after an accident practising for the Senior. A multiple champion in New Zealand who also achieved excellent results in the World Endurance Championship, at the TT he finished 2nd in the Singles race in 1974 and went one better the following year.

2004 Leader John McGuinness slows with clutch trouble on his Yamaha on lap three of the Senior, before finally pulling out at Kirk Michael, leaving Suzuki-mounted Adrian Archibald to take victory for the second year in a row. McGuinness's consolation is a Formula One-Junior 600-Lightweight 400 treble.

CHANGES

1929 The road is widened.

1935 Further widening takes place.

1973 The road is smoothed out by eliminating humps and bumps.

SPECTATING

Fields line the right of the initial lefts, while on the exit the restaurant car park provides a sizeable viewing area, with further trackside space a little way back up the course.

SARAH'S COTTAGE

A medium-slow uphill right named after Sarah Corlett, who lived here and served refreshments in the 1890s.

THE RIDER'S VIEW

Straighten the preceding left-right kinks then reduce speed on entry to the main right, although the incline itself helps. Apex this very late because again there's adverse camber on the exit, and speed is important because it's carried on up the hill and all the way along the following straight.

NOTABLE EVENTS

1953 With a comfortable lead on the last lap of the Senior, Norton-mounted Ray Amm slides off but continues, and wins after problems for team mate Reg Armstrong at Ramsey.

1965 Close to where he'll slide to earth in the Senior later in the week, Mike Hailwood is forced to retire his MV from a commanding lead on the fourth lap of the Junior. Honda-mounted Jim Redman goes on to win for the third year in a row, sealing a unique 250-350 'treble double'.

CHANGES

1930 The road is widened and eased.

1973 The road is realigned to make the bend easier.

GREG WILLEY'S HILL

Continuing up the hill, medium left-right kinks are followed by a medium-fast right-left combination.

THE RIDER'S VIEW

Hard on through the first left kink but be prepared to feather through the two rights, then hard on again through the second left.

NOTABLE EVENTS

1965 On the second lap of the Senior MV-mounted newcomer Giacomo Agostini slides out of 2nd in the wet at Sarah's. The following lap team mate Mike Hailwood does the same, although not in the same spot as commonly reported but further up the hill. Undaunted he rips off his broken screen, kicks the bike into shape, restarts it by pushing down the hill and goes on to take a famous win.

Lambfell

Still uphill, a fast series of left-right-right kinks is followed by a short straight then another right kink towards the top.

THE RIDER'S VIEW

Keep the power on over a crest before the kinks and then through them, straightening as much as possible.

NOTABLE EVENTS

1990 Having finished 2nd to the Honda of Carl Fogarty in the Formula One, Yamaha-mounted Nick Jefferies crashes out while following him on lap one of the Senior.

Cronk-y-Voddy

A fast straight with a crest in the middle.

THE RIDER'S VIEW

Flat through here.

NOTABLE EVENTS

2017 On lap two of the Superbike Michael Dunlop has forged a healthy lead when his Suzuki expires. A tight battle ensues between BMW-mounted Ian Hutchinson and Peter Hickman and Kawasaki-mounted Dean Harrison and James Hillier. They finish in that order, with only 15s separating the four of them.

CHANGES

1979 Some of the humps and bumps are smoothed out.

SPECTATING

Spectacular high-speed viewing from the fields and hedges that line the course, especially on the left. At the crossroads access is via Little London Road (B) on the right, with closed-roads access on the left via Ballaboole Road (B)

Molyneux's

A fast right after a crossroads. Formerly known as the Cronk-y-Voddy Flag, in 2013 it was renamed after 17-times Sidecar winner from the 1980s to 2010s, Dave Molyneux.

THE RIDER'S VIEW

Flat-out over another crest before the entry and through the right, except ease on a superbike.

The 11th – Drinkwater's

A fast downhill right followed by a tighter right and a medium-fast, long, double-apex left. The latter is also named after Ben Drinkwater who, having finished 3rd in the 1947 Lightweight, sadly lost his life after an accident in the 1949 Junior.

THE RIDER'S VIEW

Flat over one crest then a larger one and through the first right, then reduce speed into the the second right and into the first left apex before hard on through the remainder, including a subsequent left kink.

NOTABLE EVENTS

1932 Wal Handley crashes his Rudge in the Senior while attempting to chase the all-conquering Nortons of Stanley Woods, Jimmy Guthrie and Jimmy Simpson.

1961 Ralph Rensen sadly loses his life after an accident in the Senior, having finished 3rd in the Junior earlier in the week.

1978 On the fifth lap of the Formula One Phil Read's Honda expires, having already been overtaken on time and on the road by the Ducati of fellow returnee Mike Hailwood, who goes on to take probably the most famous win in TT history.

SPECTATING

Fields and hedges line the course on the left of the entry.

Handley's Corner

A medium left-right S-bend. Formerly known as the Ballameanagh Corner it was renamed after Wal Handley, who had an accident here in the 1932 Senior.

THE RIDER'S VIEW

A deceptively fast corner because it's blind with a cottage directly ahead. It is counter-intuitive but keep somewhat to the left of the road on entry while reducing speed, then at the last moment it opens up for a quick change of direction before accelerating hard through an unnamed, bumpy, fast left on the exit.

NOTABLE EVENTS

1991 Brian Reid comes off his Yamaha while lying a close 2nd on the final lap of the Junior 250, leaving Robert Dunlop's Yamaha to take the win from Phillip McCallen's Honda.

1999 Having won the first race, comfortable leader Dave Molyneux retires on the last lap of Sidecar B, letting in Rob Fisher for the win.

CHANGES

1954 The road is widened.

MCGUINNESS'S

A fast left in a dip. Formerly known as Shoughlaige Bridge it was renamed in 2013 after 23-times TT winner from the 1990s to 2010s, John McGuinness.

THE RIDER'S VIEW

Flat through a fast right kink on the entry and on through the left.

TOP OF BARREGARROW

A fast left at a crossroads with a church on the left, after which the road descends sharply.

THE RIDER'S VIEW

Flat through a crest before the crossroads, then reduce speed for the left before hard on again down the bumpy hill and through a right kink, the front lifting once more.

NOTABLE EVENTS

1962 Bob McIntyre retires his private Honda from the lead on the second lap of the Lightweight. Only a few months later he'll sadly lose his life after an accident in the pouring rain at Oulton Park.

2000 On the last lap of Sidecar B Ian Bell retires from a comfortable lead, handing the double win to Rob Fisher.

CHANGES

1954 The road is widened.

SPECTATING

Spectacular cornering, with Sartfell Road (B) on the right of the crossroads and closed-roads access to the left side via Ballaleigh Road (B).

BOTTOM OF BARREGARROW

A fast, bumpy left at the bottom of the hill.

THE RIDER'S VIEW

Again this bend is deceptively fast because it's blind on entry, with a cottage and wall directly ahead. Ease through a right kink on the entry, the suspension bottoms out completely in the dip, then hard on again as the still-bumpy road climbs on the exit, and on through a fast left kink.

NOTABLE EVENTS

1996 On the third lap of the Lightweight leader Phillip McCallen holes the exhausts on his Honda as the suspension bottoms out, pushing him down to an eventual 4th place, with the win taken by similarly mounted Joey Dunlop. McCallen's consolation comes in the form of wins in the Formula One, Senior, Junior 600 and Production, making him the first rider to win four TTs in a week.

2008 In the Senior leader Cameron Donald's Suzuki gradually slows due to an oil leak caused by repeatedly grounding the crankcase here. Honda rival John McGuinness goes on to take the win, but Donald's consolation is a Superbike-Superstock double.

CHANGES

1954 The road is widened.

SPECTATING

From the right of the crossroads it's possible to walk down to the bottom, which is seriously spectacular.

The 13th – CRONK URLEIGH – WESTWOOD

The 13th can be thought of as encompassing the medium-fast, downhill, double-apex right at Cronk Urleigh, followed by a medium-fast left then a longer, double-apex left at Westwood Cottage, the latter also known as Ballalonna Bridge.

THE RIDER'S VIEW

Reduce speed into the right, only making the second apex, then accelerate through the first left (late apex) before easing into and feathering through the second, where full throttle cannot be taken until the road straightens. Then flat out down the following bumpy straight, which includes a crest.

NOTABLE EVENTS

1970 Santiago Herrero sadly loses his life after an accident in the Lightweight while lying 4th on his Ossa, having finished 7th and 3rd in the same race in the previous two years. The bike was timed at an incredible 137mph and he was in contention for the 250cc world championship.

BALLACRAINE

BALLASPUR 1

BALLASPUR 2

BALLASPUR 3

BALLIG

DORAN'S BEND 1

DORAN'S BEND 2

LAUREL BANK 1

LAUREL BANK 2

LAUREL BANK 3

LAUREL BANK 4

BLACK DUB 1

BLACK DUB 2

BLACK DUB 3

GLEN HELEN 1

GLEN HELEN 2

GLEN HELEN 3

GLEN HELEN 4

GLEN HELEN 5

GLEN HELEN 6

SARAH'S COTTAGE

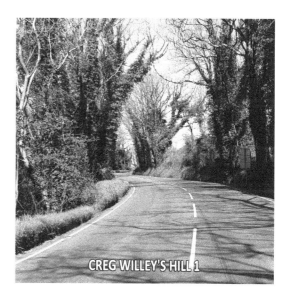

CREG WILLEY'S HILL 1

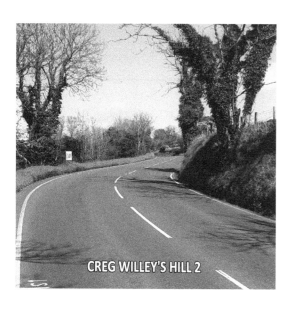

CREG WILLEY'S HILL 2

LAMBFELL 1

LAMBFELL 2

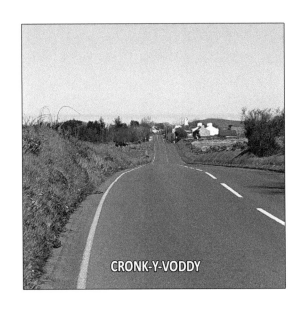

CRONK-Y-VODDY

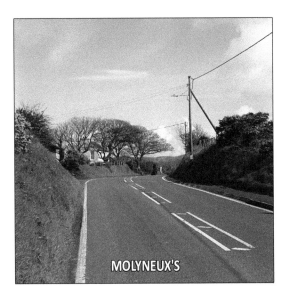

MOLYNEUX'S

11TH MILESTONE 1

11TH MILESTONE 2

11TH MILESTONE 3

11TH MILESTONE 4

HANDLEY'S CORNER 1

HANDLEY'S CORNER 2

HANDLEY'S CORNER 3

MCGUINNESS'S

TOP OF BARREGARROW

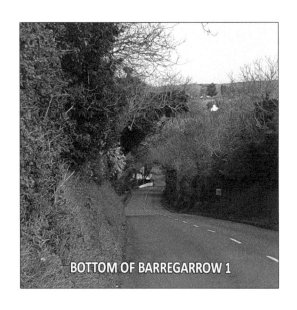
BOTTOM OF BARREGARROW 1

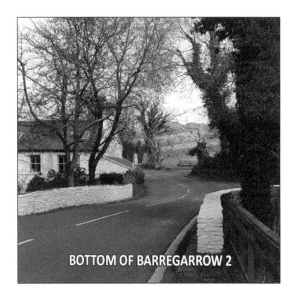
BOTTOM OF BARREGARROW 2

13TH MILESTONE 1

13TH MILESTONE 2

13TH MILESTONE 3

13TH MILESTONE 4

3 Kirk Michael to Ramsey

Douglas Road Corner

A medium, open right sweep, also known as Kirk Michael Corner, with the Mitre pub on the right just afterwards.

THE RIDER'S VIEW

This is nice and wide. Reduce speed on the entry then look for good drive on the exit.

SPECTATING

Viewing is possible from the wide junction with the A4 Peel coast road on the left. The large car park of the pub provides a somewhat more restricted view.

Kirk Michael

A fast run through the various kinks in the road as it winds through the village.

THE RIDER'S VIEW

Hard on while straightening the initial kinks, the close buildings creating a funnel effect and tremendous sensation of speed. Ease for the series of left-right-left kinks towards the end, just before the petrol station on the left.

NOTABLE EVENTS

1948 Manliff Barrington retires his Moto Guzzi from the lead of the Lightweight on lap three, leaving team mate Maurice Cann to take a comfortable win.

CHANGES

1929 The road is widened from here right through to Ballaugh.

SPECTATING

Spectacular action from Whitehouse Park, which lies on the exit of the village on the right of the first left kink.

Rhencullen – Birkin's Bend

A crest followed by a medium-fast right-left S-bend and another crest. Also named after Archie Birkin, who sadly lost his life after an accident practising for the 1927 Senior.

THE RIDER'S VIEW

Flat through a double left kink then ease before a right kink at the first crest where the bike takes off. Ease into or feather through the main right and left, then make sure the bike is upright and ease over the second crest before hard on down the hill and through two right kinks at the bottom.

NOTABLE EVENTS

1971 After the retirement of Giacomo Agostini on his MV, followed by that of fellow Yamaha riders Phil Read, Rod Gould and Alan Barnett, Dudley Robinson leads the Junior on the final lap but crashes. Yamsel-mounted Tony Jefferies takes the win.

2006 Dave Molyneux flips his outfit practising for the Sidecar, putting himself out of both races.

CHANGES

1955 The road is widened, easing the bends.

SPECTATING

From this point on access to the outside of the course is from the north of the Island only. Here it's via Orrisdale Road (B), next to which the fields on the left of the crest provide spectacular airborne action.

BISHOPSCOURT

A straight with the former Bishop's residence set back on the left.

THE RIDER'S VIEW

Flat through here, moving to the right of the road for a left kink at the end.

NOTABLE EVENTS

1966 Mike Hailwood's Honda stops on the first lap of the Junior, handing victory to MV rival Giacomo Agostini. The positions will be reversed in the Senior.

1978 Having set a new outright lap record while lying 2nd to Suzuki-mounted Tom Herron, similarly mounted Pat Hennen has a serious accident on the final lap of the Senior. Sadly he'll never race again.

DUB – ICEMAN'S COTTAGES

A fast series of kinks, named after dwellings adjacent to the course.

THE RIDER'S VIEW

Hard on all the way, this is really fast and flowing when you get it right, straightening the kinks as much as possible.

ALPINE COTTAGE

A long, fast right, named after the cottage adjacent to the house on the left of the exit.

THE RIDER'S VIEW

Ease through a left kink on the entry, then hard on again through the right.

BALLACOBB

Fast left-right kinks known also as Brough Jairg Bends or the right as Picasso.

THE RIDER'S VIEW

Flat through these, straightening them out.

NOTABLE EVENTS

2009 Nick Crowe and passenger Mark Cox have a serious accident in Sidecar 2, forcing the race to be abandoned. They will never race again.

BALLAUGH BRIDGE

A slow left at the only remaining hump-backed bridge on the course, over the Ravensdale river, with the Raven pub after it on the right. This used to be one of four commentary point until speeds rose and they were reduced to three.

THE RIDER'S VIEW

Brake hard and late into the bridge, but no heroics over it – try to minimise the time in the air, and keep the front airborne on landing. Then hard on through initial right-left kinks and on through the village, including through a long, fast, right kink on the exit.

NOTABLE EVENTS

1912 Frank Philipp retires his Scott from 2nd in the Senior, but team mate Frank Applebee still takes the win.

1939 BMW-mounted Karl Gall sadly loses his life practising for the Senior, but team mates Georg Meier and Jock West go on to take 1st and 2nd in the race. Gall won the 500cc class at the Dutch and German Grand Prix in 1937, and was German champion that same year, but in 1938 crashed in practice for the Senior and put himself out of the race.

1986 Gene McDonnell sadly loses his life after a horrific accident in the Lightweight, having achieved 5th in the Junior the previous year.

1988 On the fifth lap of the Formula One race Steve Hislop retires his Honda from 2nd, leaving similarly mounted Joey Dunlop a clear run to the flag.

1994 Honda-mounted Robert Dunlop has a serious accident in the Formula One when his rear wheel collapses. He will not return to the TT until 1997.

2006 Gwen Crellin, nicknamed the 'Lady in White' by Giacomo Agostini, sadly passes on. She marshalled at the final right kink for so long it was named after her, while her adjacent cottage was an open house for riders, mechanics and marshals – all of whose names she remembered.

2019 Chris Swallow sadly loses his life after an accident in the Senior Classic. The son of Bill and nephew of Richard, he achieved five top-six finishes in the Junior and Senior Classic, including 2nd in each of the 2012 races.

1954 The road is widened.

SPECTATING

On the right of the exit an excellent view can be had from the terrace that lines the car park of the pub, while that from the adjacent junction with Ballaugh Glen Road (B) is more restricted. On the left the junction with Cronk Road provides closed-roads access and a great view of the low-speed jump.

BALLACRYE

A fast double-apex left followed by the longest jump on the course.

THE RIDER'S VIEW

Flat over a crest on the preceding straight and on through the left, then get the bike upright before possibly easing for the jump. On a superbike ease into the left and only power on hard after the jump.

NOTABLE EVENTS

1982 With Honda's Mick Grant and Ron Haslam already retired, Charlie Williams' Yamaha expires while in front on the fifth lap of the Classic, handing the lead to Joey Dunlop. But his Honda expires at the Bungalow, letting Dennis Ireland in for the win on his Suzuki.

1993 In the Junior 250 Phillip McCallen forgets to refuel his Honda at the end of lap two and runs out. Yamaha-mounted Brian Reid takes the win for the second year in a row.

SPECTATING

Access via Ballacrye Road (B) on the left, although the hedges after the jump are pretty tall.

BALLAVOLLEY BENDS

A fast series of slight right-left-right kinks.

THE RIDER'S VIEW

Flat through here, but bumpy.

WILDLIFE PARK

The park on the left gives its name to this long, fast right.

THE RIDER'S VIEW

Reduce speed through a left kink on the entry and on into the right.

SPECTATING

Can be accessed on foot by turning left onto the old railway line towards the end of Ballacrye Road (B).

quarry bends

A fast left-right-left combination, with the quarry on the right before the final bend, also known as Gob-y-Volley.

THE RIDER'S VIEW

Possibly ease for the first left and feather until the last left-right on a superbike. Good drive out of here is another key to a fast lap as the speed will be carried all the way down the following straights, so be prepared to sacrifice entry speed and not use all the road initially – otherwise you can spend the rest of the section trying to recover your line, with a slow exit.

NOTABLE EVENTS

1989 Leading on lap two of the Junior on his Honda, Steve Hislop comes to grief. But he wins the Formula One, Supersport and Senior, and sets the first 120mph lap into the bargain. On the flip side, Steve Henshaw sadly loses his life after an accident in the Production 1300, having achieved a best of 7th in the 1983 Formula Two.

1997 Phillip McCallen crashes his Honda out of contention on lap three of the Lightweight 250, won by similarly mounted Joey Dunlop. McCallen's consolation comes in the form of wins in the Formula One, Senior and Production, giving him a treble to add to the quadruple he achieved the previous year.

2004 Colin Breeze sadly loses his life after an accident in the Formula One. In the Senior MGP he finished 2nd in 1998 and went one better the following year, also placing 3rd in the Junior, while at the TT his best was 10th in the 2003 Production 1000.

2011 Having led up until the first pit stops, Honda-mounted Bruce Anstey retires on the third lap of the Superbike. John McGuinness takes the win from Cameron Donald and Gary Johnson, all on Hondas, Guy Martin having retired his Suzuki from 2nd on the fifth lap.

CHANGES

1985 The road is reprofiled, widened and smoothed out, reducing lap times by around 5s.

2000 The last right is given a more positive camber to improve exit speed.

SPECTATING

Can be accessed on foot by turning left onto the old railway line towards the end of Ballacrye Road (B) and walking on past the Wildlife Park.

caleys

A fast left kink that in 2017 was named after Ray Caley, who ran the post office and shop at Sulby Crossroads.

THE RIDER'S VIEW

Flat through here.

Sulby Straight

A fast 1.5 mile straight that passes through Sulby Crossroads with the Sulby Glen pub on the left, then on into the village, with a fast, double right kink towards the end. The official speed trap has been situated here in recent decades, and was pre-WW2, but it was moved to the Highlander for a while.

THE RIDER'S VIEW

Flat all the way, tucking in as much as possible. Parts of this are still very bumpy, but it's much better than it once was.

NOTABLE EVENTS

1935 In an ignominious end to his TT career, Wal Handley tries to make adjustments to the rear brake of his Velocette while practising for the Junior and loses part of a thumb.

1937 Stanley Woods is forced to retire his Moto Guzzi from the lead on the last lap of the Lightweight, handing the win to team mate Omobono Tenni.

1961 With a commanding lead over Mike Hailwood on the last lap of the Lightweight, Bob McIntyre is forced to retire his Honda – although with the consolation of an incredible new record only just shy of the first 100mph lap for a 250.

1982 On the second lap of Sidecar B Mick Boddice retires his Yamaha from the lead in a close fight with similarly mounted Jock Taylor, who goes on to take the win. Two months later Taylor and passenger Benga Johansson will sadly lose their lives after an accident at the Finnish Grand Prix.

2016 On the final lap of Sidecar 1 Ben Birchall retires from the lead, handing the win to John Holden, although he has the consolation of a new lap record and a win in Sidecar 2.

2018 Kawasaki-mounted Dean Harrison retires on lap four of the Superbike, having set a new outright lap record from a standing start. His BMW rival Michael Dunlop had however been eating into his lead, and goes on to take a comfortable win.

CHANGES

1938 The road is widened.

2017 The road is resurfaced in a continued effort to smooth out the bumps.

SPECTATING

High-speed action with access to the left of the crossroads and the viewing area in front of the pub via the A14. On the right the same road leads through Tholt-y-Will and beautiful scenery to finally emerge at the Bungalow, while the Yn Claddagh side road leads up to Ginger Hall.

Sulby Bridge

A wide-but-slow right at the bridge over the Sulby river.

THE RIDER'S VIEW
Brake hard just after the kink, then accelerate out hard.

CHANGES
1922 The road is widened.

SPECTATING
A grandstand lies on the left of the entry, accessible via St Jude's Road (B), with banks lining the course before that.

NOTE that from here through to Ramsey the course is notoriously bumpy, often requiring the fastest riders to wrestle the bike and, with the front wheel in the air, steer via the footrests through the multiple fast kinks. Tiring... but spectacular to watch.

GINGER HALL

A medium uphill left named after the pub on the right.

THE RIDER'S VIEW
Ease through a left kink on the entry, then hard on again through the main left but possibly feather through another left kink on the uphill exit, watching out for a crest.

NOTABLE EVENTS
1966 On the second lap of the Lightweight, lying 2nd, Phil Read's Yamaha cries enough, leaving Mike Hailwood's Honda unopposed for victory.

CHANGES
1954 The road is widened.

SPECTATING
The pub has a large car park that lines the entry, while on its far side lies the junction with Yn Claddagh.

KERROWMOAR

A medium-slow left and double-apex right followed by a left kink known as Abbeyville.

THE RIDER'S VIEW
Possibly feather through a double right kink on the entry before accelerating briefly downhill, then ease or even reduce speed into the left. Accelerate again briefly then ease into the rights, accelerate briefly again then feather through the left kink and over a crest, then hard on.

NOTABLE EVENTS
1962 BMW-mounted Florian Camathias crashes out of the lead of the Sidecar, and when

new leader Max Deubel retires the way is clear for Chris Vincent to take a popular win, breaking the German dominance on his BSA.

CHANGES

1954 The road is widened.

Glen Duff

A fast series of kinks interspersed with straights and crests. The transport depot of the same name is on the right.

THE RIDER'S VIEW

Hard on all the way through, straightening the kinks as much as possible.

Glentramman

A medium double-apex right then slow left.

THE RIDER'S VIEW

Reduce speed into two initial left kinks and again through the rights, apexing late to keep to the right of the road for the entry to the main left. Accelerate hard on the exit as the road opens up nicely through left-right kinks.

Churchtown ~ Lezayre ~ Conker Trees

A fast section that encompasses the right kink at Churchtown, the right-left kinks at Lezayre Church, the left kink at Conker Trees (also known as The K because of the large letter painted on the tree on the left), a short straight and finally apex the right at Caravan early.

THE RIDER'S VIEW

Flat through here, although possibly just a slight feather on a superbike, watching out for the front lifting just before each left kink and for the curb jutting out at the K. Ease into the final right.

NOTABLE EVENTS

2018 Dan Kneen sadly loses his life after an accident practising for the Senior. Having made history by winning three races as a newcomer at the 2008 MGP, he moved up to the TT and achieved fifteen top-ten finishes, including 5th in Supersport 1 in 2010, and 3rd and 5th in the Superstock and Superbike in 2017.

SPECTATING

All-action viewing from the fields on the left at Lezayre Church, then all along the right of the course afterwards.

sky hill – pinfold cottage

A fast left at Sky Hill followed by a fast right at Pinfold or formerly Milntown Cottage, the now-derelict building on the left.

THE RIDER'S VIEW

Ease into the left from the middle of the road then hug the left side for the entry to the main right. Feather through it and a following left kink, then hard on again.

NOTABLE EVENTS

1996 Mick Lofthouse sadly loses his life after an accident practising for the Lightweight. Having won the Newcomer's Lightweight MGP in 1990, at the TT he finished 3rd in the 1992 Ultra Lightweight and 2nd in the same race in 1995.

milntown

Named after the house on the right, a crest over the Glen Auldyn bridge is followed by a fast right.

THE RIDER'S VIEW

Flat through here, except possibly ease for the crest on a superbike, and on through the right and all along Lezayre Road that follows. A chance to relax a little after several tiring miles of wrestling the bike.

NOTABLE EVENTS

1963 Yamaha-mounted Tony Godfrey suffers a heavy crash in the Lightweight, having lain 2nd to team mate Fumio Ito before suffering mechanical problems. He becomes the first rider to be taken to Nobles by helicopter.

2004 In what will be the last ever Ultra Lightweight race, Ian Lougher's Honda sheds its chain as he chases similarly mounted eventual winner Chris Palmer.

SPECTATING

Viewing is possible from the junctions with Glen Auldyn on the right of the bridge and Gardeners Lane on the left of the right, but both are no-through roads.

schoolhouse corner

A fast, wide left, also known as Russell's Corner.

THE RIDER'S VIEW

Reduce speed on the entry then hard on again, possibly using the lay-by on the exit if extra room is needed.

SPECTATING

Viewing is possible from the school playgrounds on the left of the preceding straight.

DOUGLAS ROAD CORNER

KIRK MICHAEL 1

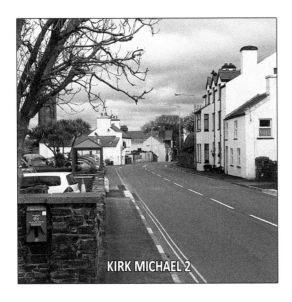

KIRK MICHAEL 2

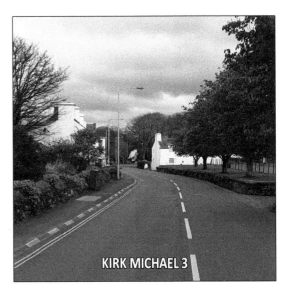

KIRK MICHAEL 3

RHENCULLEN 1

RHENCULLEN 2

RHENCULLEN 3

BISHOPSCOURT

DUBB COTTAGE

ALPINE 1

ALPINE 2

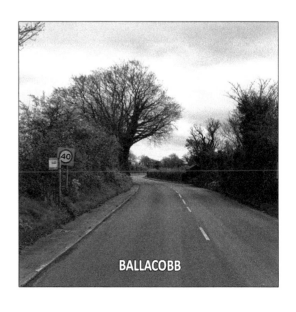

BALLACOBB

BALLAUGH BRIDGE

BALLAUGH 1

BALLAUGH 2

BALLACRYE

BALLAVOLLEY BENDS

WILDLIFE PARK 1

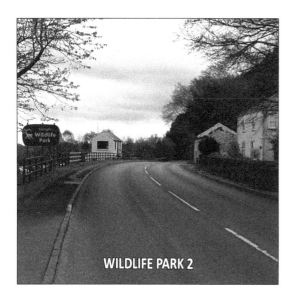

WILDLIFE PARK 2

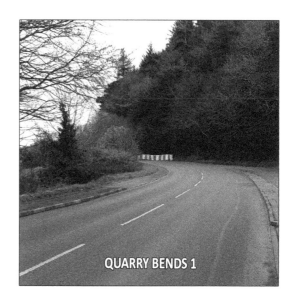

QUARRY BENDS 1

QUARRY BENDS 2

QUARRY BENDS 3

QUARRY BENDS 4

CALEY'S

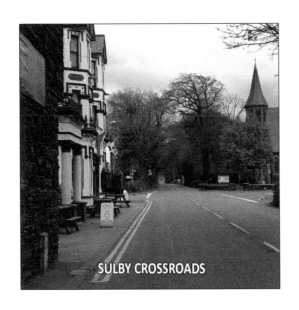

SULBY CROSSROADS

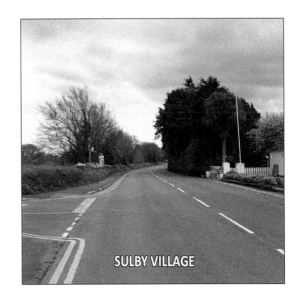

SULBY VILLAGE

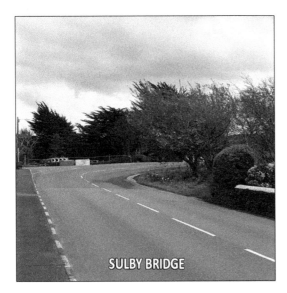

SULBY BRIDGE

GINGER HALL 1

GINGER HALL 2

GINGER HALL 3

KERROWMOAR 1

KERROWMOAR 2

KERROWMOAR 3

GLEN DUFF

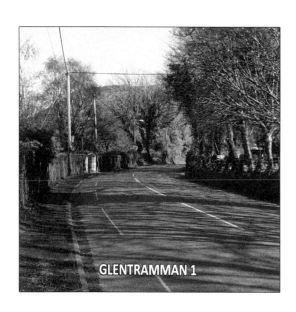

GLENTRAMMAN 1

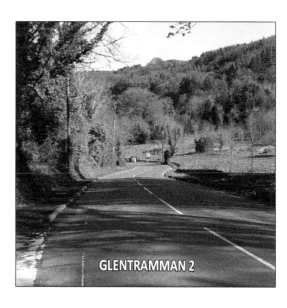

GLENTRAMMAN 2

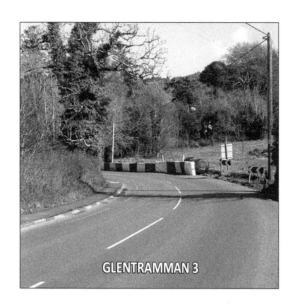

GLENTRAMMAN 3

CHURCHTOWN

LEZAYRE CHURCH 1

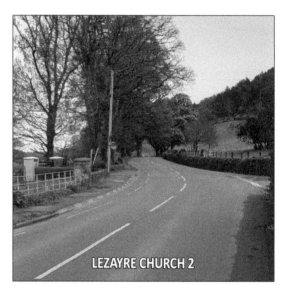

LEZAYRE CHURCH 2

CONKER TREES

CARAVAN

SKY HILL

PINFOLD COTTAGE 1

PINFOLD COTTAGE 2

MILNTOWN 1

MILNTOWN 2

SCHOOLHOUSE CORNER

4 Ramsey to Brandywell

Parliament Square

A slow right on the entry to Ramsey town, with the Central pub on the left and the Swan on the right, followed by a left kink on the exit. The subsequent straight follows Albert Road and Terrace on into Queen's Pier Road.

THE RIDER'S VIEW

Brake hard and late for this really sharp corner, then turn in late so as to get over to the right of the road on the exit and accelerate hard through the left kink, watching out for the jutting curb. The following straight is bumpy.

NOTABLE EVENTS

1911 Indian-mounted American Jake de Rosier follows up his six practice accidents in various places with another while leading on the opening lap of the Senior.

1949 Dickie Dale is forced to retire his Moto Guzzi from the lead of the Lightweight on the final circuit, but has the consolation of a new lap record.

1953 Reg Armstrong stops to replace the chain on his Gilera while vying with the eventual winner, Norton-mounted Ray Amm, for the lead of the Senior.

1971 Giacomo Agostini's normally reliable MV breaks down on the first lap of the Junior, which will turn out to be the only blemish in a series of otherwise untroubled Junior-Senior doubles from 1968 to 1972 – after which he will never return.

1973 Yamaha-mounted Mick Grant slides out of the lead of the Senior on lap three, handing a comfortable win to Jack Findlay's Suzuki.

1987 Brian Reid's Yamaha expires on the second lap of the Formula Two, letting similarly mounted Steve Hislop in for his first TT win.

SPECTATING

A petrol station forecourt lies on the left of the braking area. Then on the corner, although sadly the Central is now closed, viewing is possible from the junctions with the A9 on the left and with Parliament Street ahead. On the exit, on the right are the gardens of the Swan and another petrol station forecourt, while on the left after the kink is the junction with Waterloo Road.

Cruickshank's Corner

A medium uphill double-apex right on the climb out of Ramsey at the start of May Hill, named after the Deemster who once lived in the house on the left.

THE RIDER'S VIEW

Reduce speed on the entry, not least because although this is a steep uphill bend it's also adverse camber. Hit the first apex late and miss the second, then hard on up the hill.

NOTABLE EVENTS

2009 In the Senior leader John McGuiness smashes his own lap record before retiring his Honda with a broken chain, handing a comfortable win to similarly mounted Steve Plater.

CHANGES

1920-21 The course temporarily takes a left fork at Albert Road then a sharp right into Tower Road (which now stops short of joining Albert Road), before using what is now Parsonage Road to rejoin the modern course here.

SPECTATING

A footbridge located on the preceding straight gives access to Coronation Park on the right.

MAY HILL

A short, straight, steep climb on up the hill that levels out.

THE RIDER'S VIEW

Accelerate briefly, pulling over to the right of the road.

WHITEGATES

A medium left, named after the gates that used to lie straight ahead.

THE RIDER'S VIEW

Ease on the entry then accelerate briefly.

STELLA MARRIS

A medium uphill right, named after the villa on the left.

THE RIDER'S VIEW

Ease on the entry, although this is faster than you think because it's uphill and the camber is favourable, then accelerate briefly.

RAMSEY HAIRPIN

A slow, tight, left-handed hairpin, one of the former commentary points.

THE RIDER'S VIEW

Hard braking on the way in, although the slope helps. No heroics, watch out for the exit tightening up, then accelerate up the hill through a first right kink before feathering through a second.

1922 On the last lap of the Junior newcomer Stanley Woods lays his Cotton down on the entry, having forgotten he has no brakes left. He has already stopped to pick up spare plugs that have fallen from his pocket at the start, been set on fire during his pit stop, and stopped again to change a pushrod. Incredibly he still finishes 5th.

1935 On the final lap of the Senior and with a commanding lead Norton-mounted Jimmy Guthrie receives a signal to take it easy, on the assumption that his Moto Guzzi rival Stanley Woods would also have stopped for fuel. But in fact Woods had gone straight through and, once in the finishers' enclosure, an anxious Guthrie finally learns he's been beaten by 4s – Woods setting a new lap record in the process.

1961 On the final lap of the Junior Mike Hailwood has a commanding lead when the gudgeon pin on his AJS breaks. His consolation is to be the first man to take three wins in a week, in the Senior, Lightweight and Ultra Lightweight.

2002 The Suzuki of comfortable leader David Jefferies sticks in third gear on the final lap of the Formula One, but he still goes on to take the win.

CHANGES

2007 A one-way system from here to Creg-ny-Baa is introduced for the TT period, but not for the MGP.

WATERWORKS

An uphill, medium-then-slow, double right named after the Ballure Reservoir down in the valley on the left.

THE RIDER'S VIEW

Start to reduce speed at a left kink then on into the first right. Accelerate briefly then ease into the second, tighter right. Apex very late and apply the power with caution, it's easy to come unstuck on the exit with a steep drop on the other side of the wall.

NOTABLE EVENTS

1995 Honda-mounted Philip McCallen crashes out of 2nd on the final lap of the Junior 600, while trying to catch similarly mounted winner Iain Duffus.

2014 Kawasaki-mounted Gary Johnson crashes out while vying for the lead on the first lap of the Superstock. An eventually comfortable win for BMW-mounted Michael Dunlop forms part of a second successive quadruple, with additional wins in the Senior, Superbike and Supersport 2.

CHANGES

1939 The road is widened and landscaped.

TOWER BENDS

An uphill, medium, right-left S-bend, named after the Albert Tower that sits at the top of the hill on the inside of the track. Some sources include the uphill, medium, otherwise unnamed left-right-left combination that follows under the same heading.

THE RIDER'S VIEW

Ease into the first right, feather into the first left then hard on from the apex, up the next straight and through the second left, ease into the second right then reduce speed into the final left, taking a very late apex so as to be on the left of the road on entry to the Gooseneck.

CHANGES

2015 The road is resurfaced.

SPECTATING

Banks line the left of the straight on the entry, while the right of the course can be gained via various footpaths through the wooded slopes that rise up from Ramsey Hairpin to the Albert Tower, which lead on up to the fields at the top and right on through this section.

The Gooseneck

A slow, tight, right-handed hairpin.

THE RIDER'S VIEW

Brake hard. Nice camber round the bend but it tightens with a slight left kink jutting out on the exit. A good drive out is essential for the climb that follows.

NOTABLE EVENTS

1949 Junior leader Bill Doran's AJS expires on the last lap, robbing the marque of their first win for nearly two decades and letting Freddie Firth in for the win on his Velocette.

1975 While leading on the third lap of the Classic Mick Grant's Kawasaki sheds its chain, but at least he has finally broken Mike Hailwood's eight-year-old outright record with a lap at just under 110mph.

1997 Rob Fisher retires while in front on the second lap of Sidecar A, handing the lead to Greg Lambert who then pulls out at Barregarrow on the final lap, in turn handing the lead to Vince Biggs – who doesn't go on to take victory because veteran Roy Hanks puts in a storming last lap to register his first TT win, after three decades of trying.

SPECTATING

On the left viewing is possible from the banks on the entry, and again well after the exit. Access is possible via the Hibernia Road (B) that comes up from the A2 coast road, with parking in a field.

Centenary Bends

A medium-fast, uphill, double-apex left. As yet this name remains a proposal only.

Flat through these two except ease for the second on a superbike, hitting both apexes.

SPECTATING

On the left foot access continues from the Gooseneck, but with viewing only from the inside of the bends.

JOEY'S

A fast uphill right, formerly known as the 26th Milestone but renamed after multiple TT winner from the 1970s to 2000s, Joey Dunlop.

THE RIDER'S VIEW

Ease while straightening the slight left kink on the entry, then hard on again after the right and through another slight left kink where a white wall juts out somewhat, and on through a fast right kink.

NOTABLE EVENTS

2014 Karl Harris sadly loses his life after an accident in Superstock. A three-time British Supersport champion and then a front runner in British Superbikes in the 2000s, he switched to the TT in 2012, with a best finish of 16th in the 2013 Superstock.

CHANGES

1939 The road is widened.

SPECTATING

On the left foot access continues from the Gooseneck for those who like a decent walk, although the area lining the exit of the bend is prohibited.

GUTHRIE'S MEMORIAL

A fast-medium, uphill, triple-apex left followed by a left kink and a medium right. Formerly known as The Cutting, it was renamed after multiple TT winner Jimmy Guthrie who, having won the 1937 Junior, retired here in the Senior while leading, only to sadly lose his life at the German Grand Prix weeks later. His memorial is situated on the right side of the bend.

THE RIDER'S VIEW

Stay in the middle of the road while easing through the first left, then hard on through the next two before reducing speed while straightening the bike down the middle of the road through into the left kink. Peel into the right late and accelerate hard only well after the apex to avoid running out of road on the exit, where there's also adverse camber.

NOTABLE EVENTS

1956 Moto Guzzi-mounted Bill Lomas retires from the lead of the Junior on the sixth and penultimate lap.

1974 Rolf Steinhausen retires his Konig from the lead on the last lap of the 750 Sidecar, handing BMW and Siggi Shauzu another win but signalling the emerging two-stroke threat.

SPECTATING

On the left foot access continues from the Gooseneck for those who like an even more decent walk, although again the area lining the exit of the bend is prohibited.

The Mountain Mile

Uphill all the way, it begins with a medium left followed by a medium right through white walls. The road then jinks left and right all the way up, culminating in a fast double-apex right, again lined with white walls.

THE RIDER'S VIEW

Feather through the initial left, then hard on up the next straight and through the right except possibly on a superbike. These bends are again crucial to a fast lap because they determine the speed up the long climb through flat-out kinks that follows. Keep well tucked in all the way up. At the end remain flat through the two rights, except on a superbike possibly ease into the first. Stay out from the first apex, then hit the second one late so as to stay on the right of the road for the entry to the Mountain Box.

NOTABLE EVENTS

2017 Having already taken victory in the Superbike and Superstock, BMW-mounted Ian Hutchinson crashes while contesting the lead with similarly mounted Peter Hickman on the second lap of the Senior. In the restart, after a suspension change Suzuki-mounted Michael Dunlop takes a comfortable win from Hickman, who has the consolation of five podiums from as many races.

The Mountain Box

A medium quadruple-apex left with the shelter after which it's named on the right. Formerly the site of the East Mountain or Snaefell Gate, which was removed in 1934.

THE RIDER'S VIEW

Reduce speed and stay wide on the first apex, hit the second, stay wide again on the third then hit the fourth, accelerating hard from the second. Continue flat, straightening the fast series of right-left-right kinks that follow.

NOTABLE EVENTS

1965 Having set the first 100mph lap for a 250cc machine from a standing start, leader Phil Read's Yamaha expires on the second lap of the Lightweight, leaving Honda-mounted Jim Redman to achieve the first part of a unique, three-years-in-a-row, 250-350 double.

1970 Having set a new lap record before retiring at the NW200, Brian Steenson sadly loses his life after an accident while vying for 2nd in the Senior. He finished 9th and 2nd in the Junior in the previous two years.

the Black hut

This section begins with a fast right with a shelter on the left, also known as George's Folly after Alex George had an accident here while lying 2nd in the 1977 Senior. This is followed by a short straight then a medium-fast left sweep, with the shelter after which it's named on the right – also known as the Stonebreaker's Hut and formerly the Shepherd's Hut.

THE RIDER'S VIEW

Flat through the first right except on a superbike, hard on down the following straight then reduce speed on the entry to the left, taking an early apex for once, then hard on again.

NOTABLE EVENTS

1956 Having just inherited the lead when Bill Lomas is forced to retire his Moto Guzzi on the last lap of the Junior, the MV of John Surtees suffers the same fate, handing the win to Lomas' team mate Ken Kavanagh.

the verandah

A fast, flowing, quadruple-apex right, also known as Four Bends.

THE RIDER'S VIEW

Follow the middle of the left side of the road round the first apex, the centre line round the second, the middle of the right side round the third, possibly feathering throughout, then hit the last one and hard on again.

NOTABLE EVENTS

1934 Syd Crabtree sadly loses his life after an accident in the Lightweight, having won the same race in 1929.

1972 Leading the Ultra Lightweight on his Morbidelli TT newcomer Gilberto Parlotti sadly loses his life after an accident in appalling conditions. He has ridden because, leading the 125cc world championship, he's determined to collect maximum points. This will lead to several stars turning their back on the TT and, ultimately, to its loss of world championship status from 1977.

2010 In the re-run of the Senior after Guy Martin's crash at Ballagarey, Kawasaki-mounted Conor Cummins has a serious accident while lying 2nd on lap two, with helicopter footage showing both bike and rider flying off the side of the mountain – although he'll return to racing the following year. To demonstrate the contrasting fortunes of the TT, Honda-mounted Ian Hutchinson becomes the first man to win five races in one week, his victory in the Senior adding to earlier successes in the Superbike, Superstock and both Supersport events.

CHANGES

1971 The road is widened by cutting into the hillside.

The Bob McIntyre Memorial

A fast right kink, named after a former shelter commemorating the first man to lap the course at 100mph.

THE RIDER'S VIEW
Flat through here.

The Graham Memorial

A wide, medium left sweep named after Les Graham, who sadly lost his life on the approach to Quarter Bridge in the 1953 Senior, and whose memorial shelter lies on the right. This is also known as Bungalow Bridge. Meanwhile a further alternative name of Swallow's Sweep is suggested on a small memorial erected here for Richard Swallow, who was unbeatable on his Lawton Aermacchi in the Junior Classic from 1987 to 1991, but then sadly lost his life in a domestic incident.

THE RIDER'S VIEW
Lovely, wide and open. Reduce speed on entry and accelerate hard from about halfway round.

SPECTATING
The hills on the right are accessible on foot from the Bungalow, although the area lining the exit of the bend is prohibited.

Bungalow Bends

A fast triple-apex right followed by a medium-slow left-right S-bend, named after the hotel on the right next to the railway crossing, demolished in 1958. Set back up the hill on the right of the entry is the former Motorcycle Museum building, now the Victory Cafe.

THE RIDER'S VIEW
Flat through the first of the initial rights, then ease and reduce speed through the second and third. Stay wide through the first two, then apex the third late so as to be on the right side of the road before peeling into another late apex at the left – this so as not to run out of road while accelerating hard through the last right, to maximise speed up the subsequent climb.

NOTABLE EVENTS
1948 Having been 2nd fastest in practice, Moto Guzzi-mounted Ernie Lyons crashes on the first lap of the Senior.

1968 Phil Read retires his Yamaha on the fourth lap of the Lightweight after an epic duel with team mate and fierce rival Bill Ivy, who then takes an untroubled win. Read goes on to take the Ultra Lightweight, but only after Ivy had set the first 100mph lap for a 125cc machine before dramatically slowing on the last lap – with a strong hint of team orders.

1971 Peter Williams' Norton expires on the third lap of the Production 750 after a fierce battle for the lead with the BSA of Ray Pickrell, who goes on to win.

1972 Having demoted MV-mounted Alberto Pagani to 3rd place in the Senior, the Bungalow curse strikes Peter Williams again as his Arter Matchless expires on the last lap.

1992 Carl Fogarty's retires his Yamaha from the lead on the fifth lap of the Formula One. Honda-mounted Philip McCallen wins from Steve Hislop's rotary Norton, which hadn't even been expected to finish. A few days later Fogarty and Hislop's Senior duel becomes the stuff of legend, the latter taking the win by just 4s.

2005 Leader Adrian Archibald's Suzuki runs out of fuel on the last lap of the Superstock, letting in similarly mounted Bruce Anstey for the win.

CHANGES

1971 The road is widened by cutting into the hillside.

2017 The road is resurfaced.

SPECTATING

The electric railway from Laxey runs right up to this point, although by road it's only accessible from the inside of the course when they're closed, via the A14 that leads back to Sulby Crossroads. On the right of the S-bend lies the large car park for the café, from where the hillside above the preceding rights and even back as far as Graham's can be reached on foot. Meanwhile the fields that lie on the left of the main bend and all the way up the following hill are accessible via a footbridge on the exit.

HAILWOOD'S RISE – HEIGHT

An uphill straight with a fast right kink at the top, which marks the highest point on the course. Named after multiple TT winner in the 1960s and 1970s, Mike Hailwood.

THE RIDER'S VIEW

Hard on up the hill and through the right kink, well tucked in all the way.

PARLIAMENT SQUARE 1

PARLIAMENT SQUARE 2

CRUICKSHANKS 1

CRUICKSHANKS 2

WHITEGATES

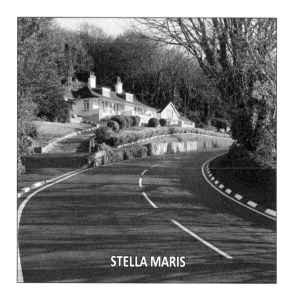

STELLA MARIS

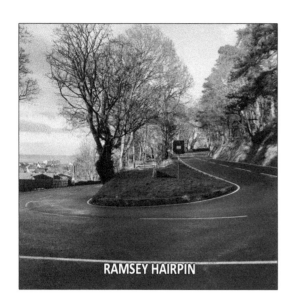

RAMSEY HAIRPIN

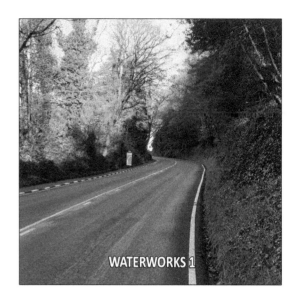

WATERWORKS 1

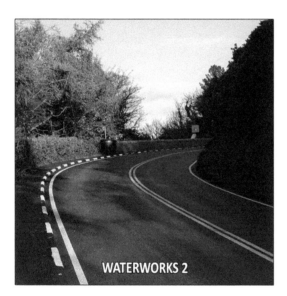

WATERWORKS 2

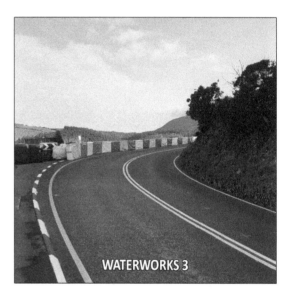

WATERWORKS 3

TOWER BENDS 1

TOWER BENDS 2

TOWER BENDS 3

TOWER BENDS 4

TOWER BENDS 5

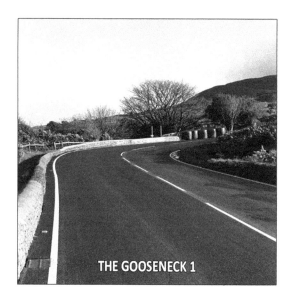

THE GOOSENECK 1

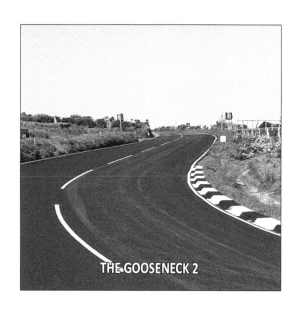

THE GOOSENECK 2

CENTENARY 1

CENTENARY 2

JOEY'S

GUTHRIE'S 1

GUTHRIE'S 2

GUTHRIE'S 3

GUTHRIE'S 4

GUTHRIE'S 5

MOUNTAIN MILE 1

MOUNTAIN MILE 2

MOUNTAIN MILE 3

MOUNTAIN MILE 4

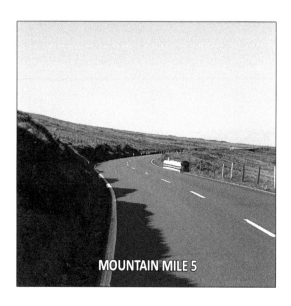

MOUNTAIN MILE 5

MOUNTAIN MILE 6

MOUNTAIN BOX 1

MOUNTAIN BOX 2

MOUNTAIN BOX 3

MOUNTAIN BOX 4

BLACK HUT 1

BLACK HUT 2

VERANDAH 1

VERANDAH 2

VERANDAH 3

VERANDAH 4

BOB MCINTYRE MEMORIAL

GRAHAM MEMORIAL

BUNGALOW BENDS 1

BUNGALOW BENDS 2

BUNGALOW BENDS 3

BUNGALOW BENDS 4

HAILWOOD'S HEIGHT

5 BRANDYWELL TO FINISH

BRANDYWELL

A medium right-left S-bend with a shelter on the right.

THE RIDER'S VIEW

Reduce speed and late apex the right so as to hug the right curb before continuing to reduce speed while peeling into the left, accelerating hard from another late apex, then hard on through a left and a right kink, but stay out from the apex of the latter.

NOTABLE EVENTS

1994 Phillip McCallen's Honda runs out of fuel while leading on the last lap of the Junior 250, handing the victory to similarly mounted Joey Dunlop.

2009 In Supersport 1 leader Bruce Anstey is forced to retire his Suzuki on the final lap, with his Honda rival Ian Hutchinson going on to take the win.

2016 Kawasaki-mounted Peter Hickman retires from 3rd on the second lap of the Senior. The win goes to BMW-mounted Michael Dunlop – who also takes the Superbike – from similarly-mounted Ian Hutchinson, who also wins the Superstock and both Supersport events.

CHANGES

1935 The road is widened by the removal of the gate.

1971 The road is widened by cutting into the hillside.

SPECTATING

Accessible only from the inside during closed roads, via Beinn-y-Phott Road (B) that leads back to the other side of the course, with fields lining the entry on the right.

DUKE'S BENDS

A triple-apex left formerly known as the 32nd Milestone, then renamed after multiple TT winner in the 1950s, Geoff Duke.

THE RIDER'S VIEW

Reduce speed into the first apex but stay wide, feather then hit the second and hard on from there, hitting the third too.

NOTABLE EVENTS

1986 On the fourth lap of the Senior Trevor Nation's Suzuki runs out of fuel, handing the lead to Honda's Roger Marshall but, when both he and team mate Joey Dunlop hit problems, similarly mounted Roger Burnett takes a surprise win.

WINDY CORNER

A wide, open, medium sweep, named because the wind blows up through a gully on the left where there is also a shelter.

THE RIDER'S VIEW

Reduce speed on the entry, watching out for the wind, then hard on through two left kinks that follow.

NOTABLE EVENTS

1921 In the Junior Massey Arran-mounted Jim Whalley suffers a puncture on the last lap while leading, having earlier taken over the lead from Howard Davies whose AJS had suffered a similar problem elsewhere. Davies goes on to win the Senior on the same 350cc machine, a unique achievement.

1967 On lap five of one of the most memorable TTs of all time, the chain on Giacomo Agostini's MV breaks during his epic Senior duel with Mike Hailwood, who was himself battling an evil-handling Honda and loose twistgrip. An exhausted Ago freewheels and pushes his bike all the way back to the pits, hoping to continue, only to be disqualified for not pushing round Governor's Dip. He throws his helmet to the ground in frustration as Mike goes on to take the win, on what everyone thinks will be his last TT appearance.

CHANGES

1921 The narrow section from here right through to the 33rd is widened and reprofiled.

2005 Further widening is undertaken as well as making the camber more positive, estimated to save as much as 4s a lap.

SPECTATING

With limited parking at the corner, viewing is then possible from the fields that line the left of the course on the entry and all the way back through Duke's Bends.

The 33RD Milestone

A medium double-apex left.

THE RIDER'S VIEW

Flat through the first part of a long double-apex right, then reduce speed through the second while taking a late apex so as to get over to the right of the road for the entry to the first left. Unusually apex this one early, then feather through the second before hard on again, including through a fast right kink that follows.

NOTABLE EVENTS

1975 On the last lap of the Junior Alex George crashes while battling for the lead with Charlie Williams, both Yamaha-mounted, the latter going on to take the win.

1999 Simon Beck sadly loses his life after an accident practising for the Senior. Having won the 1990 Senior MGP he went on to achieve five top-six finishes at the TT, including 3rd places in the 1993 Supersport 600, 1995 Formula One and 1997 Production.

CHANGES

1932 The road is widened and the bends eased.

1947 The road from here to Keppel Gate is widened with the removal of part of the bank.

KEPPEL GATE

A medium right and double-apex left. The right was formerly known as Clark's after RO Clark, who fell from his Levis while leading on the last lap of the 1920 Lightweight, but remounted and still took the win.

THE RIDER'S VIEW

Reduce speed into the right and late apex it so as to hug the right side of the road while continuing to reduce speed into the first left, watching the exit as the road falls away in a steep descent. Then hard on through the second left, but beware of a crest right on the apex.

NOTABLE EVENTS

1920 With a twenty-minute lead AJS-mounted Cyril Williams hits transmission problems on the last lap of the Junior but, using a combination of free-wheeling and pushing, still crosses the line in first place – albeit exhausted.

2009 One of the pre-race favourites, Cameron Donald crashes his Suzuki practising for the Senior, leaving him unable to race.

CHANGES

1921 The road is widened.

2009 A section of the bank on the right is removed to provide more run-off.

2014 The road is reprofiled.

SPECTATING

Parking is available on the right.

KATE'S COTTAGE

A downhill approach to a medium left. The story goes that it was given its name due to a typesetting or commentary error involving the one-time owners of the former shepherd's hut on the right, the *Tate* family. At one time it was also called Keppel Gate Cottage, and originally there was a gate across the road here to match the one at the Mountain Box.

THE RIDER'S VIEW

Ease on the way in then hard on because it really opens out on the exit.

NOTABLE EVENTS

2013 In Sidecar 1, lap one leader Ben Birchall clips the bank and retires, with Tim Reeves going on to take the win. However Birchall makes amends in Sidecar 2.

CHANGES

1994 The corner is eased on the inside.

SPECTATING

Fields line both sides of the course.

CREG-NY-BAA

A long, steep, downhill approach to a slow right, with the pub of the same name, formerly the Keppel Hotel, on the outside of the bend. A right kink on the straight that follows is sometimes referred to as Gob-ny-Geay after the adjacent farm, and also the Cutting or the Funnel.

THE RIDER'S VIEW

Hard on down the preceding descent, which includes a major crest, then hard braking. Accelerate hard from the apex for good drive down through the straight that follows, including a flat right kink.

NOTABLE EVENTS

1953 After a strong showing in the previous year's TT and the preceding NW200, Syd Lawton has a serious accident on his works Norton practising for the Senior. Sadly he'll never race again.

1968 Yamaha-mounted Bill Ivy stops on the last lap of the Ultra Lightweight before continuing, ensuring team mate Phil Read takes a pre-arranged win. Ivy nevertheless earns the plaudits for an incredible first 100mph lap for a 125.

2018 Alan 'Bud' Jackson sadly loses his life after an accident practising for the Senior Classic. Winner of the Junior MGP in 1986 and later of three Lightweight Classics, at the TT he achieved six top-ten finishes with a best of 5th in the 1990 Ultra Lightweight.

CHANGES

1954 The road is widened.

SPECTATING

With access via the Creg-ny-Baa Back Road, an excellent view back up the hill and of the heavy braking is available via grandstands on the entry and the pub balcony. Spectators can also walk a considerable distance both back up and on down the hill from here and watch from the banks on the left of the course, although not on the immediate exit of the bend. The crest on the preceding straight is a particularly popular spot.

BRANDISH CORNER

A fast, downhill left sweep. Formerly known variously as Upper Hillberry, Telegraph Hill or O'Donnell's, it was renamed after Walter Brandish crashed here practising for the 1923 Senior. There also used to be a speed trap before the corner.

THE RIDER'S VIEW

Reduce speed on entry then hard on from about halfway round.

NOTABLE EVENTS

1977 Having already secured a Formula One and Senior double, returnee Phil Read crashes his Suzuki during an unofficial practice for the Classic and puts himself out of the race.

1988 After leading and setting a new outright lap record, Steve Cull's Honda slows until it bursts into flame on the last lap of the Senior. Similarly mounted Joey Dunlop goes on to take the win.

1991 On lap two of the Formula One Carl Fogarty nearly wipes out team mate and race leader Steve Hislop, as an intermittently failing kill switch causes his Honda to cut out. They are dicing on the road but Hislop is ahead on time, and goes on to win comfortably.

CHANGES

1930 The road is widened on the exit.

2006 Considerable further widening takes place, reducing lap times by around 3s.

SPECTATING

Fields line the left of the course, accessible by walking down from the Creg or up from Hillberry.

HILLBERRY

A medium-fast uphill right.

THE RIDER'S VIEW

Faster than it might seem, not least because the slope slows the bike down through the corner. Reduce speed on entry then hard on, including through the fast left kink that follows.

NOTABLE EVENTS

1936 Jimmy Guthrie stops to replace the chain on his Norton while leading on the fifth lap of the Junior. He continues in 2nd but is stopped at Ramsey on the next lap and told to retire for receiving outside assistance, a charge he furiously denies. He restarts and finishes 5th. At the prize-giving the ACU admit they've made a mistake and award him the runner-up trophy, only to change their minds again later. He makes no mistake in the Senior, however, beating great rival Stanley Woods into the bargain.

1949 With a sizeable lead in the Senior Les Graham's AJS breaks down, but he bravely pushes in to finish 10th.

1985 Brian Reid's EMC runs out of fuel while leading on the last lap of the Junior, letting Joey Dunlop's Honda in for the win and a treble, with wins in the Formula One and Senior too. This despite the fishing boat on which he was travelling to the Island sinking, bikes and all, before he even arrived.

CHANGES

1947 The bank is cut back on the inside.

1970 The approach is smoothed out by removing some of the worst bumps.

2014 The road is reprofiled.

SPECTATING

A 200-seater grandstand on the left of the entry provides spectacular high-speed action, with access via Ballacottier Road (B). Fields line the left of the course all the way back to Brandish.

CRONK-NY-MONA

A fast, uphill triple-apex left.

THE RIDER'S VIEW

Stay in the middle of the road on the way in, easing into the first apex then feathering through the second and third, making sure you're back on the left of the road for the entry to Signpost.

NOTABLE EVENTS

1999 In the Production Iain Duffus retires his Yamaha from the lead on the last lap, handing victory to similarly mounted David Jefferies.

CHANGES

1920 This marks the first use of the modern course layout in this area, because prior to WW1 it had turned right into Johnny Watterson Lane down through Willaston, then left at Ballanard Road to come out at St Ninians where it turned right down Bray Hill.

1947 The road is widened.

1954 Further widening takes place.

SPECTATING

The Access Road leads to Johnny Watterson Lane, with viewing along the banks on the right before the junction.

SIGNPOST CORNER

A slow downhill right.

Brake hard then hard on, with the wheels right under the bank on the exit.

NOTABLE EVENTS

1925 With a commanding lead on the third lap of the Lightweight, Wal Handley slides off due to a flat rear tyre on his Rex-Acme. His consolation is to be the first rider to win two races in a week, the Junior and Ultra Lightweight – but it's so very nearly three.

2011 Cameron Donald retires his Honda from 2nd on the final lap of Supersport 2, similarly mounted Gary Johnson taking the win.

2015 In a tight battle in the Senior, Kawasaki-mounted Ian Hutchinson overshoots on the second lap. John McGuinness goes on to take the win on his Honda while Hutchinson eventually finishes 3rd. His consolation is a full return to form after his horrific Silverstone crash in 2010, just after he made history by winning five TTs in a week – although this time it's a 'mere' treble: the Superstock and both Supersport events.

CHANGES

1922 The road is widened and reprofiled.

1954 Further widening is undertaken.

1994 The corner is eased on the inside.

SPECTATING

With access via Hillberry Road, viewing is possible from the banks and from a private garden on the left of the entry.

BEDSTEAD CORNER

A medium left named after a former farmer's makeshift gateway on the right.

THE RIDER'S VIEW

Ease on the entry, watch out for the adverse camber then hard on down the next straight.

NOTABLE EVENTS

2018 On the second lap of the Lightweight 650 Ivan Lintin retires his Kawasaki from the lead, with Paton-mounted Michael Dunlop going on to take the win.

CHANGES

1953 The road is widened.

SPECTATING

The banks on the left and along the preceding and following straights are accessible via a footbridge located on the corner, which is in turn accessible via Hailwood Avenue and the Access Road.

the nook

A medium-slow right-left into the old road leading to Governor's, followed by a left kink. On the left is the Governor's house.

THE RIDER'S VIEW

Reduce speed on entry, flick right, hard on through the left then reduce speed from the exit and all the way through the left kink, swinging out wide to the left where the curb ends to negotiate the following hairpin.

NOTABLE EVENTS

1977 On the final lap of the Junior 250 Bill Simpson crashes out of 2nd on his Yamaha, similarly mounted Charlie Williams taking the win.

1990 Honda-mounted Philip McCallen crashes out of 3rd on lap four of the Senior.

2013 Gary Johnson's Honda runs out of fuel while lying 2nd in the Superbike. Similarly mounted Michael Dunlop goes on to take the win and a quadruple, claiming the Superstock and both Supersport events as well.

2015 On the last lap of the Superbike Michael Dunlop falls from his BMW in a collision with a backmarker while lying 3rd, with Honda-mounted Bruce Anstey taking the win. Dunlop plays down his injuries but won't be able to replicate his four wins in each of the last two years.

SPECTATING

Viewing is possible from the banks on the left at the end.

governor's bridge – dip

A slow, downhill, right-left double hairpin, followed by a steep rise through a slow right back onto the Glencrutchery Road.

THE RIDER'S VIEW

This is dark, slippery, tight and horrible, especially with limited steering lock, so no heroics. Accelerate briefly out of the first hairpin, ease, then hard on after the second, although possibly feathering through the right on a superbike, before hard on again over the following crest and on towards the start-finish.

NOTABLE EVENTS

1959 John Hartle drops his MV on the fourth lap of the Senior while lying 2nd, his bike catching fire and virtually burning out. His team mate John Surtees wins comfortably.

1976 Having shattered the 110mph barrier with a lap at over 112mph, and with a commanding lead on the last lap of the Senior, Suzuki-mounted John Williams runs out of fuel. Cheered on by the crowd he pushes in to take an exhausted 7th, while Yamaha-mounted Tom Herron takes the win. Williams gains further consolation when he goes on to take a comfortable win in the Classic.

1985 The chain breaks on Mick Boddice's outfit on the last lap of Sidecar A, although he freewheels across the line in 2nd and goes on to take a comfortable win in Sidecar B.

CHANGES

1922 The road is widened.

1954 Further widening is undertaken.

SPECTATING

The junctions with the A2 and with Victoria Road provide a view of the entry and exit respectively. Meanwhile playing fields lining the left of Glencrutchery Road are accessible via Dukes Avenue just before the grandstand and pits area.

BRANDYWELL 1

BRANDYWELL 2

DUKE'S BENDS 1

DUKE'S BENDS 2

DUKE'S BENDS 3

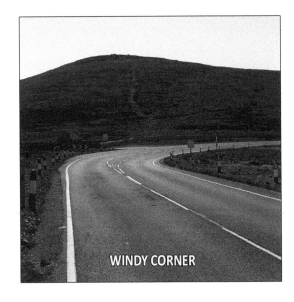

WINDY CORNER

33RD MILESTONE 1

33RD MILESTONE 2

33RD MILESTONE 3

KEPPEL GATE 1

KEPPEL GATE 2

KEPPEL GATE 3

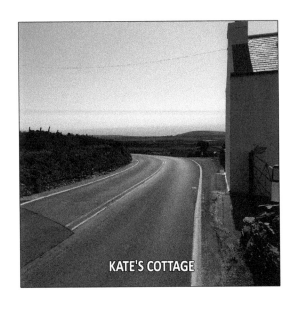

KATE'S COTTAGE

CREG-NY-BAA 1

CREG-NY-BAA 2

BRANDISH CORNER

HILLBERRY

CRONK-NY-MONA 1

CRONK-NY-MONA 2

CRONK-NY-MONA 3

SIGNPOST CORNER

BEDSTEAD CORNER

THE NOOK 1

THE NOOK 2

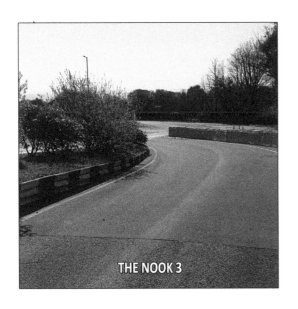

THE NOOK 3

GOVERNOR'S BRIDGE 1

GOVERNOR'S BRIDGE 2

GOVERNOR'S BRIDGE 3

GOVERNOR'S BRIDGE 4

GLENCRUTCHERY ROAD

RIDER INDEX

THE ISLE OF MAN TT COURSE

Ireland, Dennis, 52
Ito, Fumio, 57
Ivy, Bill, 73, 86
Jackson, Alan 'Bud', 86
Jefferies, David, 1, 18, 23, 34, 68, 88
Jefferies, Tony, 50
Johansson, Benga, 54
Johnson, Gary, 2, 34, 53, 68, 89-90
Kavanagh, Ken, 1, 72
Kneen, Dan, 56
Lambert, Greg, 69
Law, Con, 22
Lawton, Syd, 86
Laycock, Eddie, 36
Lintin, Ivan, 89
Lofthouse, Mick, 57
Lomas, Bill, 1, 70, 72
Lougher, Ian, 1, 18, 22, 57
Lyons, Ernie, 73
Marshall, Roger, 1, 83
Martin, Guy, 2, 18, 23, 53, 72
Mathison, Daley, 21
McCallen, Phillip, 1, 22, 39-40, 52-3, 68, 74,
    83, 90
McDonnell, Gene, 51
McElnea, Rob, 1
McGuinness, John, 1, 7, 18, 36, 39-40, 53, 89
McIntyre, Bob, 1-3, 40, 54
Meier, Georg, 51
Mellor, Phil, 22, 34
Molyneux, Dave, 22, 25, 38-9, 50
Moodie, Jim, 1, 34, 36
Mortimer, Chas, 1, 20
Nation, Trevor, 83
Nicholls, Roger, 17
Pagani, Alberto, 74
Palmer, Chris, 57
Parlotti, Gilberto, 72
Philipp, Frank, 51
Phillis, Tom, 35
Pickrell, Ray, 74
Plater, Steve, 2, 67
Quayle, Richard 'Milky', 33
Read, Phil, 1-2, 17, 39, 50, 55, 71, 73, 86-7
Redman, Jim, 1, 37, 71

Reeves, Tim, 86
Reid, Brian, 22, 36, 39, 52, 66, 88
Rensen, Ralph, 39
Richards, Ian, 33
Robinson, Dudley, 50
Rutter, Michael, 2
Rutter, Tony, 1
Sheene, Barry, 20
Shimmin, Danny, 24
Simpson, Bill, 90
Simpson, Jimmy, 1, 39
Steenson, Brian, 71
Steinhausen, Rolf, 70
Surtees, John, 1, 8, 72, 90
Swallow, Bill, 3, 8
Swallow, Chris, 51
Swallow, Richard, 2, 24, 73
Taylor, Jock, 54
Tenni, Omobono, 22, 54
Tyrell-Smith, Henry, 36
Uphill, Malcolm, 71
Vincent, Chris, 23, 56
Vine, Rob, 36
West, Jock, 51
Whalley, Jim, 84
Williams, Charlie, 52, 84, 90
Williams, Cyril, 85
Williams, John, 1, 90
Williams, Peter, 1, 20, 74
Woods, Stanley, 1, 39, 54, 68, 87

SOURCES & FURTHER INFORMATION

YOUTUBE VIDEOS

- '2018 Isle of Man Senior TT – On Board Full Lap with Peter Hickman Commentary' (the final lap on the 1000 BMW on which he won).
- 'The Morecambe Missile!! John McGuiness – TT 2015 – On Bike Lap – Senior Race – Lap 1 (on the 1000 Honda on which he finished 4th).
- 'Isle of Man TT | Learn the Course | Parts 1 to 3' (the first lap of 2011 Supersport 1 with Bruce Anstey on the 600 Honda on which he won).
- 'John McGuinness – A Legend on a Legendary Lap' (commenting on various parts of the course).
- 'McGuinness's Top 5 IOM TT Corners' (commenting on various parts of the course).
- 'TT Mountain Course Guide / Slow Lap' (in a car on open roads, good for learning the circuit, claims to include all named corners but there are quite a few missing)

WEBSITES

- www.iomtt.com/tt-database (especially the 'Meetings' section, organised into approximately twenty year segments, then by year, with full results of each race also available; a great historical source of notable events).
- www.motorcyclenews.com/sport/tt-road-races/[year]/[month] (excellent race reports as published at the time that provide a great historical source of notable events; note also 'John McGuinness's Lap of the TT', 4 June 2014).
- https://siljasttknowledge.blogspot.com (an excellent source of information on each section of the course, including written extracts from on-board footage commentary by Richard 'Milky' Quayle).
- https://en.wikipedia.org/wiki/Isle_of_Man_TT_Mountain_Course (includes background information on various names bends, course changes and so on).
- https://en.wikipedia.org/wiki/List_of_Isle_of_Man_TT_Mountain_Course_fatalities (a comprehensive listing).

BOOKS

- Harris, Nick, *Motocourse History of the Isle of Man Tourist Trophy Races 1907-1989*, Hazleton Publishing, 1990 (an excellent historical source of year-by-year results and of notable events).
- Wright, David, *100 Year of the Isle of Man TT (Updated Edition Covering 2007-2012)*, Crowood Press, 2013 (an excellent source of notable events).
- Wright, David, *Speed at the TT Races*, Crowood Press, 2017 (an excellent source of notable events and of course changes).
- Duckworth, Mick, *TT 100*, Lily Publications, 2007 (especially chapter 2, 'The Mountain Course', pp. 18–29, which includes written course notes by John McGuinness).

THE ISLE OF MAN TT COURSE

- Knight, Ray, *TT Racing*, Speedsport Motobooks, 1974 (a section by section rider's guide, replaced by...)
- Knight, Ray, *TT Rider's Guide*, Osprey, 1991 (an excellent, comprehensive guide, but now somewhat out-dated).
- Bradford, Paul, *Isle of Man Road Racing Memorial 1907-2017*, self-published, 2018 (contains exhaustive details of all fatalities).
- Copparelli, Paul and Mylchreest, Peter, *Isle of Man TT Circuit Memorials Revealed*, self-published, 2009 (a detailed reference book for memorials around the course).

SPECIFIC SOURCES FOR SPECTATORS

- www.iomtt.com/~/media/Files/2008/TT%20Raceguide%2019%2027.ashx (downloadable 'Spectator Guide' pdf with full details from the organisers).
- https://siljasttknowledge.blogspot.com.

Lightning Source UK Ltd.
Milton Keynes UK
UKHW052008080622
404109UK00001B/3